"In *Hey Cabbie II!,* the sequel to the popular 1984 book, *Hey Cabbie,* Thaddeus Logan, a former vice detective turned cab driver, has once again revealed the good, the bad, and the ugly in human behavior. Logan's fast-paced, informal style keeps the reader engrossed in the happy, funny, sad, incredulous, and sometimes raunchy tales of his passengers. As he and his fellow travelers on life's journey listen and learn from one another, Logan's empathy for his fares shines through. And his knowledge of Baltimore's history, politics and culture is informative.

The book is a fascinating sociological study. Fans of the original book will not be disappointed with the sequel, and the new book will make fans of new readers."

-Brenda Blount Saddler
Positive Self-Empowerment
Baltimore, Maryland

"*Hey Cabbie II* is a terrific, unvarnished fly-on-the-wall look at Baltimore and its residents and tourists, as told by a perceptive and hard-working man with a heart."

-Robert O. Grover
News Desk Chief (Ret.)
U.S. News & World Report

"After reading *Hey Cabbie II*, the thought entered my mind, who would know the pulse of the City any better than an experienced cab driver. Logan presents a great account of today's Baltimore. What a ride....!"

-James Waddy
Broker, Active Realty
Baltimore, Maryland

Hey Cabbie II!

HEY CABBIE II!

THERE'S NOTHING MORE REAL THAN THE STREETS

Written by

Thaddeus Logan

Edited by

Lucy J. Miller
Educator
Baltimore, Maryland

Dr. Daniel Weiler, MD
Haifa, Israel

LE.
Logan Enterprises Publishing Company
Baltimore, Maryland

Library of Congress Catalog Card Number: 2012907982
Printed in the United States of America

  ISBN-13: 978-1477621561
  ISBN-10: 1477621563

Cover photo: Downtown Baltimore, Fayette Street at Broadway
Photographer: Thaddeus Logan

In Gratitude . . .

My mother, Bernice Butler

My children, Jonathan, Monica & daughter-in-law, Jewel

My grandchildren, Jasmin, Jonathan II, Jade and Joey

Wilhelma "Billie" Garner Brown

Family and Friends

Seasoned and experienced cab drivers of the world!

To the Memory of

My Sister
Patricia Rayner Logan Williams

&

Lifetime Friend
Carroll "Bookie" Armstrong

Author's Notes

These writings feature a Baltimore City cabbie, his fares and the city he serves. They are genuine human interest stories that will keep you intrigued. The stories show the different sides of Baltimore portrayed through descriptive vignettes that allow the reader to relive his experiences. He has come to realize that people are people no matter who they are or where they reside and regardless of their pronounced prejudices or economic statuses. This is any large city USA or the World dealing with the *Haves/Have Nots* or *Rich Man/Poor Man.*

Logan, a former Baltimore City cop and vice detective, recounts his experiences as a seasoned cab driver.

T. L.

www.HeyCabbie.net

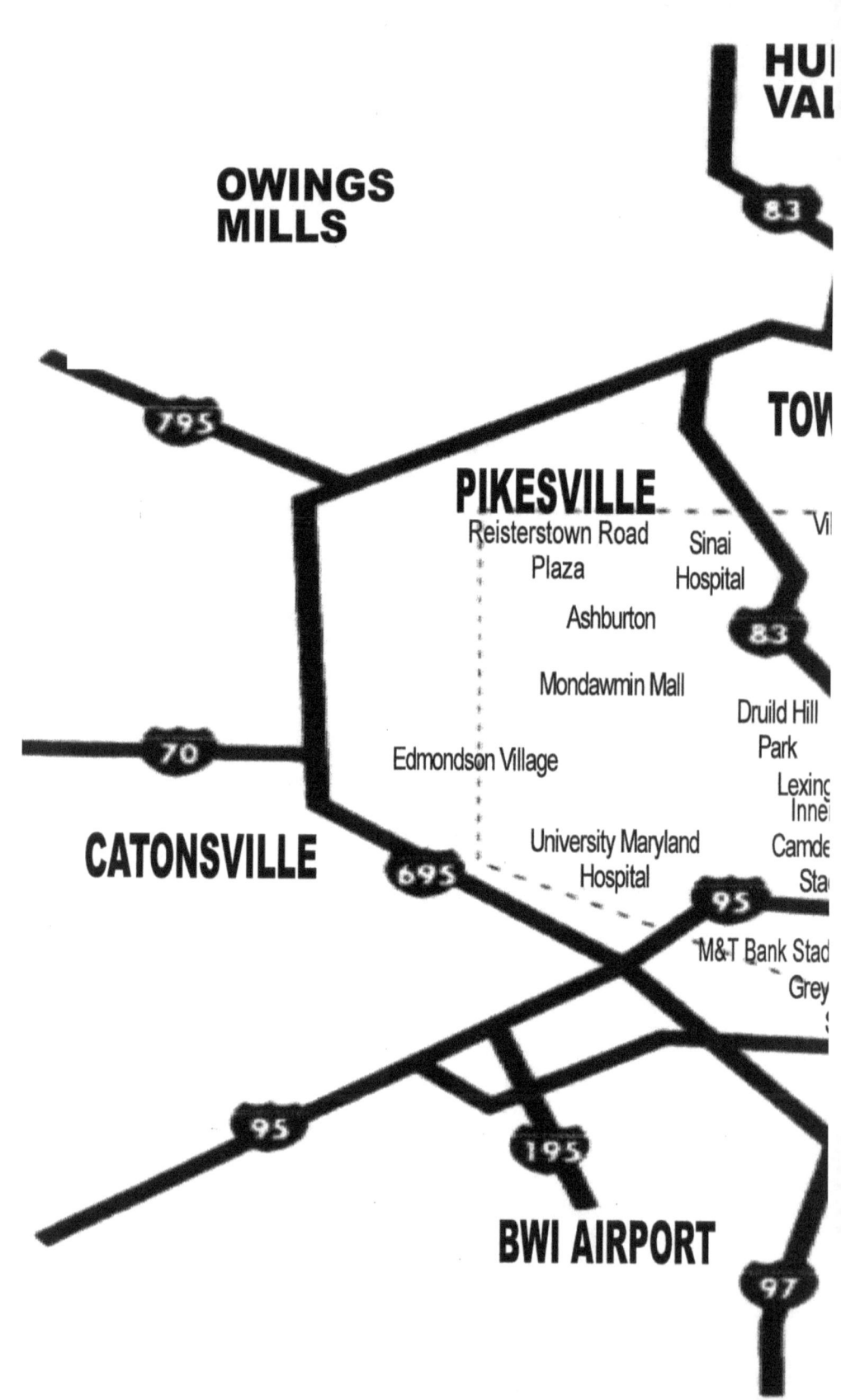

HEY CABBIE II!
"There's nothing more real than the streets ..."

Story #1

T HIS PARTICULAR SATURDAY WAS EXTREMELY SLOW. So, my decision was to sit empty beside the fire hydrant on Eutaw Street that is in front of the peanut stand at Lexington Market. A distinguished looking gentleman wearing an ascot, sporting a ponytail and looking extremely wealthy, approached the cab. "Hey Cabbie, are you for hire?" "Yes sir."

"Take me and my wife to the World Ship docked at Port Covington." Only being familiar with the Royal Caribbean, Carnival and Celebrity cruise ships departing from there, I asked is the World Ship a new line using Baltimore's Port. "No, it's one of our homes, we have an apartment aboard. This ship travels the world; renters board, disembark at will, and catch up with the ship wherever it docks. In reality it's no different than a high-rise apartment building, only being a 5-star ocean liner."

"We have an apartment in New York City and a house in Florida and would appreciate you waiting while we retrieve our luggage." Their final destination was Penn Station. "Cabbie, here's a good tip for you in addition to the fare, buy yourself one of those delicious crab cakes from Faidley's Seafood in Lexington Market." "Thank you sir, have a good trip to New York City." It must be nice, really!

Story #2

My customer, who was a tourist, contacted me by cell phone, and asked to be picked up in front of the Gallery at 3PM. A bicycle cop positioned his bike directly in front of the cab, telling me to put the gearshift in park and turn the car off. "But, Officer, my customer just called, he's coming out the door as we speak."

The customer approached, the cop told him "I can't allow you to get in because this is a truck loading zone." "Oh, give me a break, officer." He then went to the rear of the cab and started writing the ticket. You know, like why bother, I'll have my day in court.

I have been in similar situations like this before and once got locked up after being arrogant and mouthy with the cop. It just ain't worth it at this point in my life. The wise decision was to take the ticket.

The passenger was told to walk up the street about a one-half block, as the cop was busy writing the ticket. He was picked up in the bus stop on the Calvert Street side of The Gallery. "What was that all about," the customer asked. "I don't know but probably if you were to ask him, he'll say he's doing his job." As far as I'm concerned, he's making money for the City with this $52.00 fine imposed. That's an awful lot of money to a cab driver.

It's amazing the amount of stress encountered by cab drivers stemming from everybody and everywhere - the company, the public and the authorities, **but we're tough!** "Anyway, where to?" "RA Sushi Bar on Lancaster Street. Their sushi is the greatest."

"This is my first time to Baltimore. It appears to be a real nice city. Actually, I'm from California, presently stationed in

Arlington, Virginia and work at The White House." "That's great soldier!"

"I'm here in Baltimore to meet my internet girlfriend for the first time ever and Man, am I nervous! We've been talking on line for the last month." "Hopefully, you got all that question and answer shit out of the way. Just relax after initial contact, notice and compliment, especially her hair and nails. Be the gentleman that you are, don't move too fast but don't be too slow either. Trust me, you'll be just fine." "Thank you sir, I needed that bit of confidence."

Story #3
The dispatcher called for two cabs to Henderson Wharf in Fells Point. Upon arrival, no passengers were in sight, and other cabs were rapidly responding. This led me to go inside the hotel to search for the customers. They were standing next to the receptionist's desk very casually dressed. It was a party of three. The gentleman said, "Give us a minute."

Their destination was The Charleston Restaurant in Harbor East. They were purposely taking the tourist route. "What's this place about?" one of the ladies asked, "It was found in hotel's guide." "Well, it's rated among the most exclusive restaurants in the City." They looked through the windows as we approached, noticing people dressed for the evening.

They asked for other recommendations. "What's your preference in foods?" Other area restaurants were named along with their signature entrees. They still appeared indecisive but appreciated the excitement Harbor East had to offer. "Would you be interested in Italian Food? Little Italy is right around the corner." "Sure, let's go there."

They settled for Caesar's Den on High Street. The fare was

$6.00. He gave me a twenty and got out of the cab. "Sir, here's your change." "Keep it Cabbie and thank you!" Obviously, an impression was made concerning the service rendered. Literally, it pays to be polite, knowledgeable and aggressive in this business!

Story #4

I was stopped for the red light at President Street preparing to make a left turn onto Lombard Street when approached by a known downtown homeless triple amputee individual. His artificial limbs are always exposed. This intersection is known for panhandling. I was prepared to say, man today is a rough one. "I need a cab, will you take me to Baltimore and Calhoun Streets for ten dollars." "Sure, no problem, get in."

En-route I asked him what happened to his legs and arm. "I was born this way." All the while counting his beggings in this dirty, diseased looking, *scroungie* cup, more than likely found in the streets. He told me, "This is my hustle and it's damn good. Also, it keeps me with my young girlfriend because she has lots of wants and needs." I wonder if the money hustled, is in addition to his government check. He handed me balled up dollar bills and some change relative to our deal. "You're a dollar short." "No problem," searching through his pockets for more money.

He got out of the cab at Baltimore and Calhoun Streets holding a ten-dollar bill wedged in his clipped hook for a hand saying, "Thank you Man for picking me up." "No problem." "Sure Man, see you next time." He called over to one of his *hommies* and they talked.

Story #5

While cruising lower St. Paul Street in the vicinity of Mercy Hospital, Tremont Hotel Plaza's doorman was standing at the curbside of Saratoga and St. Paul blowing his whistle and motioning for a cab. He politely opened the door for the hotel's guests, which is customary, and was tipped.

"Where to Sir?" "Columbia, Maryland," I detected an accent, "Where are you from?" He told me that he was a Brazilian lawyer attending a convention here and his family tagged along to see America. He has to meet up with an old friend in Columbia and from there go on to Washington, D.C.

He began talking of American and Brazilian politics. Then he talked of President Obama being a great talker but emphatically said, "What's his plan? People need to work in order to be self-sufficient in a stable environment." He also talked of the world being in serious trouble. "Today, the whole world's in turmoil." saying, "Like how is the world gonna come out this mess?"

He said his President and Obama became friends after the G-20 Summit. "They really have nothing in common, education or otherwise. Obama is a constitutional lawyer and his wife is also a lawyer. My President is a drunk and his wife is a housekeeper. Like's what in common between these two statesmen?" My reply was, "Maybe they just wanted to form an alliance between the countries."

Also, he talked of the President's daughters making their own beds in the White House, saying, "That eleven year old girl of mine in the backseat won't do a damn thing unless she's paid. My wife and I are trying to instill more responsibilities in our children. We definitely failed somewhere. We've employed maids; they come cheap in Brazil and perform most of the household needs."

"Crime is very high in my country. Bandits will stick you up at the red light, demanding your watch, jewelry and money while stopped. You better not be driving a convertible; it will be seized. Women and children of the rich are known to have been kidnapped and very high ransoms are demanded. Some captives have been killed." "Well Sir, we're not there yet... Hopefully, never!" Anyway, it was a good fare and he wanted transportation to the airport the following day.

Story #6

The cab was dispatched to Iggies Restaurant in the 800 block N. Calvert Street. This is a small cozy restaurant on the southern edge of Mt. Vernon with outside tables. Three young ladies beautifully dressed for the evening entered the cab. "Where to Ladies?" "Johns Hopkins University, 33rd and North Charles."

These girls were quite pleasant, talking of their girlfriend who apparently was having the ball of her life. This chick has a boyfriend with a late model BMW convertible and occasionally is chauffeured in his limousine. They said, *MONEY!*

Recently, they went on a dinner date in his chauffer driven limousine. The chauffer escorted her from her apartment building to the limo where he was standing outside waiting. He greeted her with a light kiss. The chauffer opened the car's door while he entered on the other side.

The atmosphere was perfect with dim soft amber lighting, romantic music by Whitney Houston and pebbles of red roses spread over the seat. The chauffer popped the cork from a good bottle of red wine, pouring them a drink. They had dinner at The Prime Rib Restaurant, later went to his place and watched silent movies.

The lady seated rear right shouted *"STOP"* throwing her hands up in the air, stomping her feet on the floor expressing her excitement and enthusiasm. Lightly, I pulled on my right earlobe, indicating that I was listening and joined their laughter. The happiness they expressed for their girlfriend was quite charming!

Story #7

It has been a tough week, which contributed to my projected goal being off. My normal work week is Monday through Friday and some Saturdays. The Ravens were playing Pittsburgh this Sunday at M&T Bank Stadium and working the game will make the week.

There is lots of love and admiration for the Ravens' home games, but as a cab driver, it's murder. I attend a few games yearly for clarification. The problem is not taking the fans to the stadium. They stagger in from everywhere and by many different modes of travel.

The madness starts at the beginning of the fourth quarter. The police and traffic enforcement officers start barricading most of the incoming streets leading to the stadium. Hamburg and Ostend Street Bridges are completely closed off and used for pedestrians only.

There is no cabstand and the police will not let cabs stage on Russell Street adjacent to the stadium. They keep you moving, which force the drivers onto Interstate #395. Either passengers have to approach cabs while stopped at the red light or drivers pull over unnoticed by the cops for pickup.

This is senseless; fans who are cab riders must make complaints to the Public Relations Division in The Mayor's Office to correct this situation. How can we even be considered as a tourist/convention city if the City does not provide accessible taxicab stands at Camden Yards and M&T Bank Stadiums?

*This same situation occurs on Preakness Day at Pimlico Racetrack, just on a much larger scale. This single-day event is the City's crown jewel. **There are well over 120,000 people in attendance from all over the world. Just imagine the magnitude of this crowd dispersing after the Preakness race and being confronted with severe transportation problems.** People are stranded in an unfamiliar neighborhood and the cops are merciless ticketing cabbies for picking up passengers on Northern Parkway. Many cabbies have refused to work the Preakness! Drivers are told to stage on Pimlico Road at Belvedere Avenue. This is about five good city blocks from the infield's tunnel entrance and at least 6-8 blocks from the clubhouse. People come to these events to party and for their enjoyment, not to be hassled with public transportation problems when leaving the venue. **It is crucial that cabs have staging in close proximity to the clubhouse and tunnel for the convenience of the patrons. This situation can definitely leave an unfavorable taste to attendees, especially out-of-towners. Many would appreciate it if the City would revisit this situation between police, cabbies and patrons***.

Anyhow back to M&T Bank Stadium - after being forced onto I-395 and finding Martin Luther King Boulevard's access ramp to Russell Street closed due to the stadium's event, I had to drive three miles to get back to the stadium by driving over the triple bridges, then across Hanover Street Bridge, north on Waterview which leads back to Baltimore Washington Pkwy/Russell Street.

Fans were literally running up the Russell Street Bridge when cabs came into sight. My doors were locked, right front window partially down, being determined not to take any short fares. A black man about 45 years old partially dressed in Ravens gear pulled on the locked door. "Where to Sir?" "Laurelville around Cold Spring Lane and Harford Road in Northeast Baltimore." "Get in."

Once seated, he talked of being a seasoned Ravens ticket holder for years. "This has been one hellava experience; it's been extremely difficult to catch a cab. The racism from many of these drivers is just unreal. They would say they're on call once my destination was revealed and immediately picked up whites when approached. I feel totally disrespected, like less than a human being."

"Sir, it can be economics apart from race. Unfortunately, that's the driver's call. Unfair practices can always be reported to the Public Service Commission of Maryland." Believably most Blacks think it's race alone. We had a good sports conversation for the remainder of the trip. The fare was $23.00 and I was given a $5.00 tip. "Thanks for picking me up, Go Ravens!"

Story #8
A young black teenage girl who appeared to be in need of transportation was standing at the curb's edge with children when I was pulling out of the gas station located at 33rd and Greenmount. She approached the cab, got in and asked me to drive around to Giant Foods to pick up her groceries.

The trunk was popped and the young lady requested help loading the groceries into the car. Her cell phone rang moments later and was answered. She stopped everything, totally ignoring that I was there helping her, and engaged herself wholeheartedly in this phone conversation. My assistance came to an absolute halt and I returned to the driver's seat of the cab and turned the meter on!

Anyway, Giant was out of food carts, their customers were waiting impatiently for her to unload her cart. My passenger noticed me back in the cab and finally finished loading her groceries into the trunk. The fare had advanced to $4.60 when she finally got seated.   No respect, no apology, no acknowledgement for the delay!

My God, cell phones are the biggest distractions ever! It seems like everyone's preoccupied, including me at times.   Like, who is actually focused?   Many people answer their phones whenever and wherever, whether signaled audibly or by vibrations.   Pedestrians and automobile drivers are observed continuously around the City talking, texting or scrolling their hand held phones and actually paying no attention to their surroundings.   There appears to be limited exceptions. Although, Maryland has a law on the books concerning hand held phones when driving, many are not abiding including some City employees.

Story #9
Sometimes, using a little instinct and knowing human trials and behaviors, you cruise in and around the City's hotspots in search of a fare. The Meyerhoff Symphony Concert Hall was letting out.   While turning onto its passenger drop-off pad, there stood, this young lady about 35 years old, looking beautiful in her black full-length dress waving and smiling. She took a seat; her destination was the Broadview, at 39th and University Parkway.

She said, "The concert was absolutely excellent, I must say!" I detected an accent, "Where from?"   "My home is Madrid, Spain. If I were there, boarding the public transportation would have been used in place of a cab. It's not a problem; everyone uses it, even those that have cars."

"Europe's public transportation is excellent. It's efficient and the service is always on time. Those with money, also utilize the public transportation systems as well. People who have automobiles minimize their use. Their houses are much smaller than those of Americans!"

"The rich live in the cities and many prefer walking and cycling. They have much love for large metropolitan areas and wouldn't have it any other way. They seem to enjoy life's pleasurable pleasures! The cities are so much more cosmopolitan with their activities and vibrations, like New York, Washington, D.C., Chicago and San Francisco. They're alive! Vacations are referred to as holidays."

"Sixty is the retirement age in my country. Europeans don't seem to be as cliquish as Americans are. Don't get me wrong, America has an awful lot to offer. I sincerely believe that Americans and Europeans could learn so much from each other's cultures."

Story #10

Extended holidays are good business from college students, especially Thanksgiving. Cabs stage at all colleges and universities in the days prior to the holiday. Loyola University is a biggie. Two students, a male and female, made eye contact with me to pop the trunk. Their luggage was extremely heavy for a four-day school break, knowing that many students take their dirty clothes home for laundering.

While driving to Penn Station, the man was discussing with his companion how he got stopped by the cops for drunk driving and having fake identification. Consequently, he was locked up.

He had discussed the situation with one of the University's officials and was told that 90 percent of the students there possess fake identification cards and those that don't should not be here! He was told no "C" grades by his parents because of this troubling situation and that he must maintain a "B" average to keep all privileges. Then he told his companion that he would be sailing his boat around Boston's Bay over most of the Thanksgiving weekend.

Many minors ride cabs to the bars in Fells Point and York Road, especially on Halloween and St. Patrick's Day. They are often observed and overheard quizzing each other relative to the fictitious birth dates on their fake identifications. It is obvious and overlooked by many, including numerous merchants and City agents.

Story #11
Sometimes cabs staging in line at Pennsylvania Railroad Station is the best thing going in town. At least, you are guaranteed a fare once becoming number one cab. The trip could be long or short, that's the chance you take. Better jobs come from either the radio or cabstands. There is also that moment of relaxation and shutting the motor down. Sitting, *"really ain't my thing,"* I prefer making a monetary goal, then charging after it.

It amazes me when sitting in the taxicabs' train line on St. Paul Street observing people either coming from Penn Station or the Bolt Bus and how they wait patiently to catch the Charm City Circulator, the City's FREE bus to downtown Baltimore and Federal Hill. The majority of folks appear to be quite capable of affording public transportation. It's believed this project was created during the tenure of former Mayor Sheila Dixon. We are in the most serious recession of my time and actions such as this certainly are not helping to strengthen Baltimore's economy.

In recent years, the taxicab business has become tough! Believe me transportation is still as viable as ever, but we have just been invaded from everywhere. Numerous institutions such as hotels, churches, colleges, universities and hospitals have created their own transportation services. Our own cab company started sedan service years ago. Transportation for the handicapped had been handled exclusively by cab drivers. Now sedan service transports the handicapped with just a small percentage of the business going to the cabbies. The taxicab side had been the frontrunner for various divisions of the transportation company and its previous owner. The transportation company has rapidly expanded since the acquisition.

There was a plan a few years ago to make Penn Station the transportation hub of the City. The bus depot was to be located on the north side at Lanvale Street between Charles and St. Paul with a connecting bridge over the railroad to the station. This was a great idea for the surrounding neighborhoods and the City, having trains, buses, local transportation including light rail and taxicabs centrally located. Actually, for the cabbies, longer fares stem from Greyhound Bus Station located at Russell and Haines Streets in Southwest Baltimore.

The busybodies of the immediate neighborhoods got together privately and politically and stopped this project. Their argument was that heavy commercialism would harm the cultural arts and entertainment persona of Station North.

Where was the hue and cry of the neighborhoods concerning the creation of the open-air Bolt Bus stop in the 1600 block St. Paul Street that is functional 24-7? This situation creates massive problems, double parking, crowded sidewalks with passengers and a trash nuisance, in addition to blocking the bike lane traffickers.

The Penn Station transportation hub would have been the economic engine for much to come! Where were the visionaries? Hey, the forward thinking leadership of the late William Donald Schaefer was definitely needed in this situation or the fearless guidance of Governor Martin O'Malley who reversed the speed camera legislation that was voted down. The efforts would have been tremendous for the surrounding neighborhoods. Many new businesses would have opened and flourished in addition to the development of upscale neighborhoods. Look at Washington D.C.'s success around the Metro Stops of 7th and H Streets and 14th and U Streets. This is just another misguided, misfortune for Baltimore!

Oh well, the taxi train line is moving, soon I'll be number one cab; hope to get a good fare. People were lined up in front of the taxicab line waiting their turn for service. My cab was the third vehicle in line. It was obvious that for the cab directly ahead and operated by a foreigner that his passenger would be an elderly black woman on a cane. He was talking on his cell phone when moving up and the automatic protective shield was observed being closed. It certainly doesn't take long for some foreigners to practice discrimination once they become indoctrinated into the American system.

My customer was a well-dressed African American man wearing what appeared to be a Joseph A. Bank or Brooks Brothers' suit, towing a black business travel suitcase and a computer case securely attached to his luggage.

"Where to Sir?" "Cabbie, I grew up here, my family relocated to Seattle, Washington after my father's transfer from the Post Office came through. There are many fond memories of this

City. Cabbie, that was 50 years ago, I was only 14 years old then. My company's national convention is in D.C. and I had promised myself to visit Baltimore on this trip. I'd appreciate hiring your services for a while. By the way, I'm John and I see from your hack badge that you're Thaddeus." "Sure, no problem, where do we start?"

"My old neighborhood was around Fulton and Baker. We lived in the 1500 block Mckean Avenue. Let's go there first, and then to Mondawmin Shopping Center, Provident Hospital and the black tennis courts in Druid Hill Park."

"Let me geographically route this tour. John, would you prefer being flat rated or do you want me to run the meter?" We agreed on a fair price for three hours of service. Interstate #83 north was traveled to the North Avenue exit west. He commented on the new townhouses around the intersection of North and Eutaw, saying that he has made a good living off real estate in Seattle.

After riding a couple blocks further up North Avenue, he observed a sharp contrast in people and activities around McCulloh Street. Grown men of all ages were hanging around on corners and in front of liquor stores; some even had their pants drooping down with their underwear showing. Cars had to maneuver around people jaywalking, there were many boarded up houses and a heavy police presence. "What are this City's population and its percentage of Blacks?" "We are 65% of Baltimore's 650,000 people." "The percentage of Blacks in Seattle is about 12% and it's rare to find them gathered in clusters." "Well John, welcome to Baltimore."

"Where are we?" "North and Pennsylvania." "I remember this intersection well. Like studying at that Enoch Pratt Branch #17 library regularly, attending the Met Theatre, seeing first run films. My family also dined occasionally at

Wilson's Restaurant."   Some of those businesses have been razed for Baltimore's subway system and the Penn North Subway Station.   Remaining are the library and the old Tickner's Jewish Funeral Home building now consisting of small businesses, including the Department of Welfare and other City agencies.

We made a left turn from North Avenue onto Fulton.   The scene was wild at that intersection.   The homeless worked motorists with their hand printed signs at the traffic light. "Man, I don't use the 'N' word, but I ain't never seen so many niggers milling around, doing absolutely nothing in my life." "John, what junior high did you attend?" "The school's name was Charles Houston, number 181 on Calhoun Street." "I hate to blow your mind, the building is still standing but it's been rehabbed for senior citizens to live in."

He was totally devastated by the time we turned onto Mckean Avenue, especially after passing a curbside R.I.P (rest in peace) memorial on Fulton Avenue with teddy bears, candles, balloons and wine bottles surrounding a tree.   John said, "What's that about?" "It's the scene of a murder. That's how street killings are memorialized in the ghetto." "Oh!"

Then we went on to find that where he once lived had been reduced to a vacant lot with weeds three feet high.   As a matter of fact, the whole block was a vacant lot but for the exception of three houses left standing. All the houses on the other side of the street where boarded up.   "This is just unreal." "John, ghettos are developed through blind neglect over time, man and man alone created this type of devastation." "But, Thaddeus, this! Where are these people?" "Who knows, but city records should be able to uncover ownership of the vacant lots and houses."

"There are over 30,000 vacant houses and lots in this City." "That's unbelievable!" "John, it's like there're two different Baltimore's. There is the highly progressive section where there's rebuilding and re-growth and gentrification, with people who consider themselves environmentalists and then what you have been observing since leaving I-83. We share similar cultures, one flag; but it's like we are two different nations. Some of us definitely need to become more SERIOUS! Although, we are the majority in Baltimore's population you would never know it. We lack in homeownership and are quite sparse in the business sector." "Thaddeus, what are the largest black businesses in Baltimore City?" "Well, John, outside of the black church, it would be the beauty parlor, the barbershop and funeral homes." "Huh!"

After parking the cab, we both took a tour of Mondawmin Shopping Center. This mall is one of the major shopping centers in Baltimore. It has been rehabbed three times. The Maryland Transportation Authority (MTA) has a major transportation hub here with buses from the north and south feeding into its Metro Station. Many people frequent this mall from everywhere. Some of the stores are kind of low-end reflecting the demands of what the people from the neighborhood want and can afford. "Thaddeus, I must say this place's appearance is first class, without a doubt!"

"Oh yeah, you mentioned Provident Hospital. It's been closed for years." One of the country's few and our only black-owned hospital did not stay open long after building its new facility on Liberty Heights Avenue. Bon Secours Hospital occupied the building briefly but now Baltimore City Community College uses the building.

Druid Hill Park is a place of beauty with its rolling hills and reservoir. It's great for those who want to get away but stay within the City. People are either by themselves or in groups.

They can be found participating in various sporting activities, exercising, being entertained, dog walking or just cooling out.

The tennis court that was used by Blacks during segregation is still in use; it now has a spectators stand. Years ago, one was able to drive completely around the reservoir. You could park directly above I-83's 28th Street exchange and observe the interstate curving in a southerly direction with downtown as its background.

The park also had a lover's lane that has been closed off in addition to other back roads. The zoo was once free. There was a rental charge for rowboats at the boat lake. That area was fenced in years ago, including the entire zoo. The boat lake has not been operational for years. Now, the zoo charges an admission fee and is owned by the state.

"Those apartment buildings located directly across from Druid Hill Park are absolutely magnificent. They appear so stately overlooking the lake." "What's the name of this street?" "This is Druid Park Lake Drive. It is a major cross-town thoroughfare. Depending upon your apartment's location, views of the north and south of the City are absolutely breathless. This could have been one of the City's gold coasts!" "What happened?" "Who knows?"

John went on to say, "I did mention that I'm in the real estate business?" "Yes sir." "Waterfront, lakefront and golf course properties are worth lots of money just about everywhere.

"Well, Thaddeus, this was one great learning experience! Hey, I'm staying at Admiral Fell's Inn in Fells Point. Here's more then what we agreed on." "Thank you, Sir!" "Let's have a drink and bite to eat after I get settled in." "No problem, there's a nice little outdoor tapas restaurant and bar next to the hotel. I'll see if they have an available table outside."

Story #12
Once again, my cab was next in rotation on Penn Station's taxi stand. This white woman about 25 years old entered, her destination being Thames and Ann Streets in Fells Point. She sighed with relief after being seated comfortably. Disclosing that she was a lawyer and worked 12 hour-long days for a senator in Congress. "But, tonight, I'm going to visit my boyfriend. Actually, I live in Ellicott City."

"This commuting and working is no joke. We all put in at least 12 hours every day, including the Senator. All of the lawyers that work for the Senator except me are from his home State. I'm quite fortunate, huh?"

She said, "If you watch C-Span, the people seated directly behind the Congressmen and Senators do all the leg work and research. I saw President Obama as Senator but never as President. Both were sworn in as Senators on the same date. This is my most interesting undertaking ever, seeing the legislature at work and its different processes." We both agreed that these experiences are invaluable.

"This job goes beyond all my expectations, ever, not knowing where this experience will lead. It certainly will enhance my resume." "I bet your parents are thrilled to no end. Well, great challenges are out there depending upon your assertiveness and aggressiveness. You'll be all right, just continue to be your own best advocate."

Her boyfriend greeted her with a pleasant welcome, having red roses probably purchased from a Fells Point street vendor. He was standing in front of John Stevens Restaurant upon our arrival. That's sweet and romantic!

Story #13
The dispatcher routed cab #1914 to Johns Hopkins Hospital's Wilmer Eye Clinic located at Broadway and Jefferson Streets. This clinic is known worldwide for its research, treatments and improvements to people's vision. Their patients are global.

My passengers walked to the curb after seeing me coming around Broadway's traffic circle. The lady gave assistance after noticing the man having trouble finding the door. They were en route to another doctor's appointment in the First Mariner Bank Building located at Boston and Clinton Streets.

The lady's cell phone rang. It was her son, she told him that, "Daddy's eye condition isn't as bad as we had assumed. The doctor said your father is 90% blind in the left eye and 60% in the other with no peripheral vision in either. He has tunnel vision only. Some sight may return in time."

The son then asked his mother, "Will dad be able to drive?" Laughing inwardly, saying to myself, "This man couldn't even find the doorknob. How in the hell is he ever going to be able to operate an automobile? Where was the son's head after hearing his mother reveal the medical report?" She said, "We're gonna have him tested by the DMV if he insists on driving."

Well, I sincerely hope that I'm nowhere in sight if and when he ever decides to operate a motor vehicle.

Story #14
While cruising in the 1600 block Thames Street and being noticed by an Asian woman who ran into the street and crisscrossed her arms above her head drawing my attention.

Four fashionable young ladies (two Asians and two Americans) entered the cab from all angles when stopped.

Their destination was the Red Star on South Wolfe Street. The gal who sat up front was a dish, wearing a mini skirt, black tights, high boots and long matching scarf. While en route, one of the ladies in the backseat threw a box of rubbers to the lady up front. She jumped back projecting astonishment saying, "You know that I'm not that type of girl!" We all got a good laugh as they were thrown back. "Hey, looks like this is going to be fun tonight for someone, huh." Again, we laughed.

Story #15
The fares onboard were here to see the Orioles play the Yankees. There is money to be made when the O's play New York or Boston; most of these games are a sellout. This particular game was called because of rain. These people had been partying at Pickles Pub that is located directly across from Camden Yards when flagged. "Take us to Mother's in Federal Hill."

New York and Boston are cities of serious wealth. Consequently, most of the games played in their cities are sold out and quite expensive. It's like our City becomes transformed into theirs during these games. Major transportation carriers profit, the downtown interstates are jammed and hotels get what they demand. The Inner Harbor streets become impossible to maneuver. Patrons wait patiently in line for restaurant service. Liquor establishments in the Harbor's vicinity do well. Their hometown team's paraphernalia is proudly worn and abundantly displayed. Baltimore is definitely their playground during these games.

Two young black women about 25 years old approached me as the fare was getting out of the cab at Mother's. They asked was I hacking and would I take them to The Gallery for $5.00? "Miss, this is a licensed taxicab by the Public Service Commission of Maryland. What's with running the meter? I'll guarantee you that it won't cost $5.00 and will prove it to you, but first give me that five you were going to give the hack man." "No problem, sir."

She said, "Those foreign cab drivers have been ripping us off big time. That's why many Blacks pass up most available cabs! Some are nasty and disrespect you as a woman. Most make out they don't know where they're going and will take you the longest route possible. I've even been put out of the cab blocks before my destination because an argument had ensued."

"Miss, I'm extremely sorry that this happened! I know what you talking about and have heard others relate similar incidents. Encounters such as this can be reported to whatever cab company was hailed and the Public Service Commission. Anyway, your fare from South Charles and Cross Streets to Calvert and Pratt is $3.80." "Thanks Sir, have a good day."

Story #16
I was sitting illegally on the Calvert Street side of The Gallery when approached by a black man requesting service. It was a short ride to Lombard and Greene Streets. He talked about how he appreciates Christmas gifts but many times the sizes are wrong. I found that this sweater was purchased on sale that ended last week. This same sweater cost me $15.00 additional dollars." "Well my Man, at least someone thought of you." We got a good laugh!

Story #17
This recession is absolutely unreal. They say unemployment is somewhere between 9-10 percent nationwide. This does not include the underemployed. It seems like about 40% around here. Most industrial businesses left Baltimore years ago. Today, even those who are highly qualified are not guaranteed employment in this global market.

You would not believe the percentage of cab rides that are subsidized by the government. Many people in this City are actually penniless. Some become that way less than a week after exhausting their monthly check. Really, *the haves* and *have nots* are quite prevalent in Baltimore.

Like, what happened to cash money, aside from becoming somewhat of a cashless system? It is unbelievable the number of $5.00 to $10.00 credit card charges for cab rides. Charge work is constantly growing in this industry. Many businesses are reversing the credit charge percentage for purchases back to the consumer. The question has been asked many times is that practice legal?

Lately, everything has become tough! It appears from what's seen through the windshield that America is decaying right before my/our eyes. Many businesses in one way or another are involved in downsizing with either their employees or their benefits. Some have even closed their doors forever. It is believed that sooner or later groups of people are *gonna* stand up and say enough is enough. Like, what's going on - demanding answers. Don't be surprised if violence erupts.

People are having difficulties paying their bills from month to month. Some have hit rock bottom. We're definitely in trouble. Solutions are needed almost immediately for these poor idle people willing to work. There is no American dream in sight for many without a functional productive society. Third world status is rather imminent!

Baltimore has suffered from cutbacks for the past 30 years. To my recollection, it all started in Baltimore City under Mayor Schaefer's administration with the closing of various firehouses that added insult to injury when computers were replacing the human workforce. In recent years, employees have been reduced in most city agencies including police, fire and the sanitation departments. Even the City's school system was not spared.

We are sliding down the bell shaped curve rapidly. America's highest quality of life seems to have peaked if what has happened in Baltimore City is relative to our nation. It's like the uncertainty of our country has plummeted since 9/11. The country just celebrated that tragedy's 10th anniversary.

The Occupy Wall Street spread to Baltimore is thoroughly understood. Corporate greed, control and government corruption have had an extremely significant role in the demise of various aspects of our City. Baltimore was once a striving blue-collar city with one of the country's largest seaports. Private industries' contracts contributed to Baltimore's wealth and prosperity. People's jobs were relatively secure. This enabled many to accomplish their American dream. For most, that's a house and car in secure neighborhoods with a good school system for their families.

This professionally dressed middle-aged black woman was noticed standing next to a medium size cardboard box in front of the World Trade Center. She flagged after the traffic light changed. The trunk was popped and assistance was needed. Her destination was Upper Park Heights in the vicinity of Clarks Lane.

She appeared to have been crying when entering the cab and apologized for her demeanor. "Mister, I just lost my job after putting in some 20 years of service. The company is relatively small, strapped for cash and needed to downsize. My seniority was low compared to others in the firm. So, consequently, I was forced to take a buyout.

"The offer is good but Mister it won't last forever. That in conjunction with unemployment and my savings must do for now! I'm 50 years old, had a high-level position and salary was close to the six figure range. The money will last for a minute but I must formulate priorities in addition to long and short termed plans.

"My biggest expenses are condo and car notes. Which is heavy," she said laughing and crying simultaneously. "Oh, my God, just what am I going to do as a single woman facing such a dilemma?" All, I could do was listen, it was saddening. Then to top it off, she talked about having to ready herself for the job market at her age. "I have excellent job skills and experiences in my field but my asking price may be prohibitive. You know, it's a global market and these firms want individuals they can mold and cultivate. It's gonna be tough, real tough!

"This bombshell is undoubtedly the heaviest experience *EVER*! Knowing that I'll grieve for awhile but once accepted and recovered I'll give it my ALL and if no jobs are to be found then the focus will be on self employment as a consultant in my field." Miss, I have to admire your courage and strategy for attack. Sounds like you're saying *plan your plan, then work your plan.*"

Story #18

One of my regulars called who lives in upper Roland Park. She always books the cab in advance and requested service to BWI Airport for herself and girlfriends. These ladies use my service regularly, are well up in years and live what appears to be a real good life. They are extremely independent and two are widowed.

They are serious socialites, play bridge regularly, belong to book clubs and exercise at Curves. They also, travel extensively throughout the year, primarily to New York, Florida and sometimes to Europe. Once a year they get together for a reunion with their girlfriend for years who has a cottage in Cape Cod Massachusetts.

They pack a light suitcase and are always ready when called for. It takes no more than a half hour for pickup from three different locations. They talked the normal girl talk and the latest gossip from their circle once comfortable and relaxed in the cab.

On this particular day, they were speaking glowingly of one of their girlfriends who has a new *boo*. These ladies are rather refined in nature. One lady said, "He's tall, handsome and debonair. He looks great in his clothes and that gray hair is always styled. Really, he appears to be quite charming. But, you know, after talking to him, apparently, he seems to be the type that wouldn't have a book or magazine in his house." I laughed to myself. She certainly sized him up!

Story #19

This particular week cab business has been extremely good because of the blizzard. There was no other reason for this increase. It reminded me how this business was in the old days when ridership was plentiful, heavily crossing all cultures and classes of life. Today, one must strategize or use other methods in making money, such as sit, sit, sit on various cabstands throughout the city, or take radio calls dispatched. The old street flags from ordinary citizens are primarily nil.

Anyway, the Saturday that followed the blizzard was routine. The trips were short, business was slow but food stamps were out. So off to Mondawmin Mall in Northwest Baltimore, my focus being Shoppers Food Market because good seasoned cab drivers always follow the money trail to obtain their hourly, daily and monthly goals. Knowing these experiences from the mall would be wild because food stamps were put in distribution after the blizzard. But one must do what one has to do!

No cabs were waiting on the Shoppers stand. Grocery shoppers appeared cold and angry waiting for available transportation. Their shopping carts were maximized. Cabs were scooped up by shoppers like a bunch of seagulls in search for food - spot, dive and snatch. Two ladies ran towards my cab while one stayed with the grocery carts when noticing that the cab was empty. The trunk was popped while moving in their direction.

My meter was activated when they start loading up the trunk. It took awhile with my assistance. These big boned heavy young ladies finally got into the cab, by this time the meter was reading $3.80. "Hey, it starts at a buck eighty. You put the meter on and we haven't even moved." "Lady, my service started when you begin loading the trunk from those two food carts." Unfortunately, knowing from experience that a tip is out of the question, you'd be lucky to get what the meter reads. "Oh, you're one of those kind, huh." The lady said no more, reclined in the seat and started sucking her thumb.

En route to Fulton and North Avenues, all side streets were either snow blocked or had just one lane for both inbound and outbound traffic. "Why didn't you go down that street cab driver?" "Don't you see that car stopped and those two twelve foot snow mountains at the opposite intersection?" They kept saying what you should have, could have done, whatever. There was just no reasoning with these unreasonable people!

They never gave me an exact address, just the intersection of North and Fulton Avenues. Not knowing what they meant and all the while noticing this fool on the traffic island in the middle of North Avenue hollering, "The house is over here." Because of the blizzard causing very heavy traffic and detours, the meter read $7.80. Under normal circumstances, it would be about $5.00. The fare said, "Give me my fucking change," while I was fumbling around purposely in search of two dimes in my change box. "Don't be cursing at me Lady!" That really set off the fireworks, calling me everything including my mother's son. You learn to shut up to ignorance after years of experience; it just ain't worth it, period. This abuse continued while they unloaded their groceries. My trunk was slammed shut, of course that was expected. "Adios, you ungrateful bastards."

Relieved, thinking this was the end of the episode. But, after jumping into the westbound traffic on North Avenue, I noticed the abusive lady and man running in my direction hollering "Stop Stop!" Knowing that something had to be left on the backseat, I looked around and observed her pocketbook. Well, it was my turn after absorbing all their shit. The rear right window was lowered automatically while driving and her pocketbook was thrown from the cab to the curb. All the while keeping a keen eye on the traffic light at North and Monroe wanting it to stay green…Thankfully it was!

28

Story #20

The cab was hailed by a black teenager at the intersection of Monroe and Pratt Streets. There he nodded to a lady later learned to be his grandmother who was kind of slumped over and leaning against the wall of Bay Island Seafood. She was assisted to the cab, requested the front seat and was observed toting an oxygen tank. The lady was panting heavily for breath and told her grandson to adjust the tank to its fullest capacity, only to realize that the tank was completely empty. Saying to myself, "Oh my God."

The grandson replied, "There's a fresh tank at the house," and they lived close by. It was a short ride to a small street off the 2300 block of Wilkens Avenue. She said, "Mister step on it," and told her grandson to rush in the house, hook the long cord up to the tank and stretch it out the front door and not to forget the nitro pills.

At the house, the teenager moved like a snail. I shouted at him, "Boy, hurry up, move it," he turned around with a hard stare and looked at me. A neighbor helped me get the lady from the cab as the grandson returned with the items requested and a folding chair. Her eyes were as wide as saucers when she flopped down in the chair. The fresh oxygen rejuvenated her immediately. "What an ordeal," saying to myself, sighing with relief!

Story #21

Our bus had just pulled into downtown Baltimore's Greyhound Bus Station, returning from a trip to Atlantic City. My daughter and I decided to take a cab, making me a passenger, which is a rarity. Cabs were lined up for service. The taxicab starter told us that the fifth cab was available. Our driver was assisting a fellow cabbie when we approached. We were advised to take a seat.

After being greeted, he was told our destination was in the vicinity of Morgan State University. The route we desired was Calvert to 25th Street and straight out Loch Raven Boulevard. He programmed his personal GPS, checking the route before proceeding.

It was a good ride uptown. He was not on the phone, the music was decent and the cab was exceptionally clean. In conversation, he told us he was from the Caribbean. The meter indicated the final fare being $18.40 when we had reached our destination.

"What's our fare Driver?" His reply was, "$19.90." I'm aware of a fifty cents off the meter night surcharge after 9 PM, which brings it to $18.90. But, where's this other dollar coming from? "The dollar is for being dispatched to Greyhound." "Your posted Public Service Commission Rate Card only indicates a dollar extra when called for service and nothing about any money, period, for cabs staging at Greyhound Bus." He appeared to withdraw his demand when challenged.

"Driver, it's tough to judge a book by its cover. You really never know who you are transporting. I'm not a part of the Public Service Commission but I am an owner/operator of a taxicab and medallion here in the City. This is one of the main reasons why people with lesser means find other modes of transportation.

"I've found that if you present yourself well, be polite and give good service; the tip is inevitable, at times it may be beyond one's expectations. Thank you for the ride, here's $22.00 for the service."

Story #22
The computer dispatched me to the Dollar Store located in Mount Clair Station at Pratt & Carey Streets for a taxi access fare. This is a government-sponsored program that entitles the elderly, sick and handicapped to taxicab transportation twice daily with a limit of $20.00. They are required to pay $3.00 on a $20.00 fare and up to four people can ride. The fare appeared to be waiting impatiently when approaching. The man, a bit older than his female companion, was tipsy. "Take me to the check cashing place where the subway station is on North Avenue." "Sir, you're taxi access customer, my computer indicates transportation to the 2400 block Francis Street, knowing that you're aware of taxi access requirements. That being exact locations of the trip on both ends." "Yeah, but I don't know the address on North Avenue." "Sir, you're not even close with this Francis Street address." "No problem, North and Pennsylvania it is."

The $3.00 service fee was paid on a $12.00 taxi fare to North and Pennsylvania. There additional service was requested. "Sir, cash only," the meter was tripped while waiting. He returned about 5 minutes later, "Take us to Park Heights and Virginia Avenues. Hey, but I need a drink first, stop me at Sugar Hill Bar on Whitelock and Druid Hill."

The young lady stayed in the cab. She started talking about the dude, saying how she couldn't stand a drunk. "He's all right when sober." Figuring her to be along for the ride after refocusing my rearview mirror and knowing that checks were out; I thought she probably will milk this guy for as much as possible.

She then told me in discussion how tough it has gotten to find a mailbox in the Pimlico section of town. The drug dealers have played a major role in addition to our economic situation. They hide drugs in the mailboxes by anchoring them down

31

with a long string and retrieve them when needed. They're staying one-step ahead of the police. In addition, many have been set on fire. Finally saying, "Times are absolutely unbelievable."

The drunk came out the bar with purchase in hand, veered several yards to his left, pulled out his stuff in broad daylight and took a piss. The cops in a marked vehicle stopped for the traffic light, noticed but did nothing. They just rolled on.
He took a swallow from the bottle once seated in the cab. She also took a hit and then said, "Baby, I'd sure like a new pair of shoes. Let's stop at Mondawmin." "Maybe later baby, I'll buy you two pairs of shoes depending how good that pussy is." "I'm gonna get those shoes, Cabdriver step on it, please." The fare was paid to the exact penny, "Like where's my tip for waiting?" "Here Man, handing me a dollar."

Story #23
The cab company employs an individual at the Pennsylvania Railroad Station referred to as a starter. His job is to assist passengers and their luggage into the next available cab in addition to maintaining order with the drivers.

The starter approached me in my cab and asked would I accept a credit card fare to Aberdeen, Maryland. "Sure," with a laugh, "put him in here." He appeared to be the business type and his luggage was placed in the trunk. The passenger was told the fare will run in the neighborhood of $75.00 to $80.00 and his credit card needs to be processed within Baltimore City's Metropolitan Area prior to arriving in Aberdeen in order to get an approval number. He said that wouldn't be a problem. "Here's my card, process it for $100." "Thank you very much, Sir!"

He later said, he was on the Acela, Amtrak's top of the line train, having a business conversation on his cell phone and missed the station call for Aberdeen. He became frantic, running up and down the train looking for the conductor. He was not to be found until the train was moving towards Baltimore's Penn Station. The conductor told him Aberdeen's announcement was made and for those departing to move to the rear car. The Train Master at Penn Station offered a hop to get back to Aberdeen on a northbound train but time was a factor.

It was imperative that he get to Aberdeen quickly to review his notes and have briefings from colleagues prior to their 9PM meeting. He wasn't sure if taxicab services were available in Aberdeen so that's why a cab was taken from Baltimore's Penn Station. He thanked me for transporting and was told that we are helping each other.

His product was selling 401K's to large companies and corporations. He had been on the road in four major cities the last five days. Saying, "Man it gets old after awhile. But, my relief comes this weekend catching up with my family at a Massachusetts ski resort." "That's great; hopefully, you'll relax and enjoy yourself."

Story #24
It was one hot sweltering summer afternoon. The cab was parked in Fells Point at the foot of Broadway and Thames Street. My air conditioner was on full blast, man was it hot! Also, this is a water taxi stop. There are always lots of people lined-up waiting for the water taxi during the summer weekends. On this particular weekend, lines were exceptionally long and knowing that a fare would soon come, if for no other reason than being exposed to that hot sun.

A white couple approached, requesting transportation to the Intercontinental Hotel on Light Street. They appeared to be seniors, lived in sunny Southern Florida and decided to vacation in the Baltimore/Washington Metropolitan Area. The vicinities of Miami and surrounding cities are breathtaking. Thinking about retiring there if my social security and savings allow. You know money is always a factor.

"How is it to continuously live in a warm climate? Many people like seasons and look forward to the change." "Oh, Florida is nice after living in Virginia, 65 to 70 degrees is really cold. Being dirt poor then as a child, no heat in the house, waking up freezing and remembering snow gathering inside the windowsill. Having to go to school hungry, holes in my shoes and a rope for my belt. That was then, this is now - Florida is definitely the place for me.

"My wife and I did rather well for ourselves, owned and sold an 18-hole golf course prior to relocating. We now live in Palm Beach and our backyard is a golf course." I know that golf courses are second to waterfront properties in the real estate market.

"How are the Marriott Retirement Villages?" "They're really nice and have excellent assisted living programs." Told him that I consider myself a young vibrant senior who loves the beach, partying and riding in convertibles. "Well, you'll be right at home Brother!"

"Here we are Sir, the fare is $11.00." "You were interesting, keep the twenty." "Will my services be needed for transportation to the airport?" "Sure pick me up tomorrow about 8AM. What's your cell phone number?" "Thank you Sir, see you then."

Story #25

The run to BWI Airport is approximately 8 miles from M&T Bank Stadium on Russell Street. Once there, we have to deadhead back to the Baltimore because our boundaries for picking up passengers are within the City limits only. Seasoned cab drivers will check Greyhound Bus, the Hilton Hotel and University Hospital right off Russell Street when returning to the City.

The dispatcher called for cabs on the stand at University Hospital. My vehicle was number one. The taxicab starter signaled for me to pull up to the main entrance and I was told to pop the trunk. A lady seated in a wheelchair appeared frail, weak and breathless while being assisted to the car. She was given home care instructions from her nurse as they hugged and said good-bye. The luggage and wheelchair were placed in the trunk.

She asked, prior to starting, "Do you accept credit cards?" "Sure, no problem, but cash is preferred!" "I live in Crownsville, MD, will you take I-97 South to MD Route #178." "Sounds good to me, no problem Miss." It's good money, being about 25 miles from the City, thinking to myself.

This lady was a couple years my senior. She had had a lung transplant and recently suffered a relapse. We talked of the good times back in the 1960's and 1970's. Reflected how relaxed society was on sex and drugs. This woman had a whisper like voice that was *kinda* sexy. We exchanged our names and had a very good conversation while riding down the road.

"Oh! Here's our exit," that being Exit #5 off the interstate. We traveled about 1½ miles on Route #178, and then turned onto a side road that ran parallel to the Severn River. Her residence appeared serene. The Severn River Bridge was in clear view when pulling into the driveway. It was magnificent!

A middle age man, riding a John Deere tractor was mowing the lawn. "That's my oldest son, who's an investor, recently relocated to Maryland. My other son who lives in California grows pot legally for the state." "Oh yea?" "Yea, I'm not proud of his profession but that's what he does."

The son who was mowing the grass never acknowledged us, which threw up a red flag. Like, what's going on here? Did this lady sign herself out the hospital? The fare was paid; she gave me a decent tip.

You would think that her son would be happy to see his mother and would have stopped and assisted. He never even said hello. It was a struggle for the lady, she had to stop and take deep breaths before being seated in the wheelchair. Then, there was the luggage! But, her controlling personality was sensed when getting her from the cab to the house.

Her 90-year-old mother, who lived in the basement apartment, came upstairs and demanded to see her daughter's discharge papers. They were in order. My calling card was given to the passenger after having refreshments. I wished her all the best before leaving. My thoughts are confused from not knowing all the circumstances.

A call was received days later, requesting my services for an entire day. We agreed on a price after strong discussion. Her house was 25 miles from Baltimore City; pickup time was 9AM, the following day. My normal workday is 11AM to 7PM; sometimes my daily routine becomes disturbed. I was offered coffee before our day started, and then she insisted that her car be driven instead of the cab. Don't forget, there's a wheelchair involved.

We started off at this swanky beauty salon in West Annapolis. The return time was pre-arranged. I killed time by having breakfast at the Greek Diner on West Street in Annapolis, and then took a brief tour of the city before returning to the salon. My passenger was handled carefully and seated gingerly in the wheelchair with all eyes focused on me. Like, saying to myself, who am I, Morgan Freeman driving and assisting Miss Daisy?

We had lunch at California Pizza in Annapolis. Minor errands were run, in addition to getting the car washed and stopping at Staples. She personally wanted to go inside at these different locations. That meant retrieving the wheelchair and rolling her around wherever.

My evening ended around 5:30PM, man was I tired. My age must be telling on me! It's easier just dealing with passengers in and passengers out all day then this. Prior to leaving, arrangements were made for the following week.

She was picked up in time for her 9:00 AM appointment at Baltimore/Washington Hospital off Route #100. I noticed that she was breathing a little heavy. This was the first of her weekly visits after being discharged from University of Maryland Hospital. They checked her out, saying everything was fine. Once again, she was helped to the wheelchair.

The next order of business was Target in Annapolis. The shopping was done by me with a list while she waited in the car. She called while I was in Target saying the transplant unit at University Hospital said for her to go to the nearest hospital ASAP. That was Anne Arundel County Hospital. They had detected something in a lab test.

The hospital was notified in advance, priority treatment was setup by University Hospital. The necessary paper work was completed by me as they worked on my passenger. The family was notified. They took care of me before leaving the hospital. It was later learned that her potassium level was extremely low. That evening she was taken by ambulance to University Hospital.

My services were needed a week later. She was recouping at a nursing home in the vicinity of Ritchie Highway and Route #10. Her pickup time was 8:30AM. However, first, she wanted me to go to her Crownsville home and get her personal car and wheelchair. This request was given careful thought as silence came over me. Thinking, this was a terrible imposition prior to picking her up. Her home was 25 miles from Baltimore City.

She was flat out told that I am a cab driver and that is the service that I'll provide. Really, I could not imagine how much time was needed to perform this early morning task during rush hour. She then said in a high-pitched tone, that I'm paying you and this is what I want!

"I'm sorry but you'll have to find someone else." I refused to compromise, although the money was good. This job was wearing me out and the role portrayed was not me. It certainly wasn't my character!

Story #26
Cab 1914 was dispatched to Stadium Place on 33rd Street. This site was once Memorial Stadium, home field for the Baltimore Orioles and Colts. The old stadium was later razed and has been replaced by senior citizen buildings, an athletic field and a YMCA.

This was a taxi access job; two elderly ladies were waiting. One requested the front seat because of her handicap. Her walker affixed with a seat, basket and cane was placed in the trunk along with some grocery bags. Their destination was the 200 block of North Monroe Street. Once seated, the lady up front fumbled around in her pocketbook for the taxi access card and $3.00 for the fare, dropping a good portion of her purse's contents on the cab floor. Of course, my assistance was needed!

They enjoyed the ride across town. The lady in the back said that she could not remember the last time seeing the Druid Hill Park's Reservoir. She asked, "Is it still lit up at night and did they ever solve the case concerning the lady found dead in the fountain?" "Miss, that's one of Baltimore's mysteries, the case is well over 20 years old and no Ma'am to both questions."

"Driver, she lives on the 3rd floor, take us to the side entrance on Monroe Street." To my surprise, the lady up front was giving her girlfriend a lift home because she had no money. It was asked, "How are you getting home," while assisting her friend to the door with groceries. "Well, if I can't get another cab on this taxi access card, then I'm gonna have to catch a cross town bus." The girlfriend thanked her and said, "You can't manage any bus in your condition. What's wrong with you?"

My computer was checked indicating the Monroe Street taxi zone was empty. She was instructed to call the cab company after borrowing her friend's cell phone, while I booked into that zone on my computer. I received the call moments later. She was lucky, damn lucky!

We talked, the lady had various illnesses including diabetes, recently had a big scare while riding the bus to play bingo out in Anne Arundel County. She did not take her insulin that particular day because her sugar reading was good earlier. But, she became tired; fell asleep on the shuttle bus and the driver could not wake her. Consequently, paramedics were called, transporting her to the Baltimore/Washington Hospital. Later, when awakened, she was told that her sugar reading was fourteen. "My God Miss, it's a wonder that you're alive." "Yeah, I know, I often think about that!"

"Miss, your friendship to this lady has to be invaluable, but relative to this situation, your own well-being needs careful consideration accordingly. I know for a fact that climbing three flights of stairs would have been difficult or impossible. Where is your cell phone?" "It's home on the kitchen table." "Suppose, your diabetes started acting up while waiting?" "I hear you, Mister."

"Really, *were you thinking*, do you realize that more than likely you could have been sitting out here in the cold waiting for hours on your walker while your girlfriend is in her warm and toasty third floor apartment?" It appeared that the girlfriend has a selfish trait. God knows when a cab was coming in that neighborhood.

Story #27
The economic status of my customers varies from rich man to poor man. Many slices of life are experienced on any given day. This particular day, one of my regular riders called who resides in one of Baltimore's senior citizen buildings in the vicinity of Johns Hopkins Hospital. Primarily, the trips are short. They need transportation to various medical facilities due to their debilitating health problems and age.

They appreciate me being punctual like themselves, giving respect and listening intently to their problems. The average trip is $8.00. They will pay $15.00 for the service and company. Most fares are paid with their mobility taxi debit card. This is a partially funded federal program for seniors with medical conditions or the handicapped managed by the MTA.

My computer indicated after swiping the card that $20.00 remained on the books, knowing that a return ride was needed. He paid the usual $15.00. His wife seated rear right was assisted to the curb first. Then help was given to the elderly gentleman who was seated rear left. Traffic was waved around while struggling to free his left foot that was jammed under the seat. Once out of the cab, his balance was steadied with the help of his cane and me.

The old man noticed 3 pennies spaced a part in the gutter when attempting to step to the curb. He could not resist the temptation, dropped the cane to the ground and damn near toppled over on his face to retrieve those pennies, which probably cost more to produce than they were worth.

This situation was funny but serious and contributed to me being overtaken with a feeling of guilt! But I soon snapped out of it after thinking that not one blessed dime was ever solicited over and beyond payment for the services rendered. His method of extending money as bait for good dependable service worked to the advantage of us both.

Story #28
The dispatcher put out a call for cabs to the National Aquarium. A black woman about 25 years old with a child waved when the cab was sighted. They wanted to go to Holiday Inn Express, at Gay and Fallsway.

The radio was tuned to the Michael Baisden Syndicated Radio Talk Show. The topic for the day was planned parenthood. She said, "That never works." "Why so, Miss?" "My husband and I tried everything and every position humanly possible for me to get pregnant when ready for a baby. I just couldn't conceive.

We later separated, had sex and I became pregnant immediately. Driver, we were both in the military at the time and reconciled." But later she found out that he also impregnated this white woman. So she booted him out! The children are the same age, give or take a month. It's to my understanding that she doesn't want the child.

"He wants me to get back with him for our child's sake and to adopt his outside baby." She said, "Never, even if I wanted him back. First of all, I'm not getting back for no children. Then, even if I would think of considering, I'd never adopt the child that was conceived when we were attempting to reconcile. I would rather adopt a totally unknown child before his." "Yes, I hear you, Miss."

Story #29
While stopped in traffic for the red light at Pratt and South, this cute, what appeared to be a lesbian couple, had been sitting on the bench at the bus stop in front of Harbor Place's Pratt Street Pavilion. They approached from the curb lane and asked was I working? "I certainly am." "Will you take us to Morgan State University's Blount Tower? That's the dorm on its south campus, Sir."

One was of fair complexion with long blown hair, black mini skirt revealing endless legs, wearing a white see through blouse, braless showing nipples and sporting very high platform shoes. I must say she looked good! Her friend wore a straight brimmed wide baseball cap with neatly cropped short braids, white tee shirt, blue jeans, new tennis shoes and no makeup. She was pretty much titless.

Actually, they were very polite, saying 'Sir this' and 'Sir that' when talking to me. They became extremely involved and expressing their love while talking. The stud continuously pushed her lady friend's hair out of her face while being eyeball to eyeball to one another when in conversation. Finally, they kissed and it was overheard from the stud saying how delicious she smelled and that she couldn't wait to get her in bed. They hugged, rubbed and kissed on each other up until the cab approached their dorm. The fare was paid, I was given a decent tip and they hurriedly ran into the dorm hand in hand. All I said to myself, I would have loved to have been the fly on the wall! It is what it is.

Story #30

It is always a good thing to have a fare waiting when the one on board has reached their destination. Like, let's keep the money flowing. Anyway, after my passenger on board got out at the welfare building located 3000 E. Biddle Street another one entered. He appeared to be about 40 years old, his destination being 200 E. Lafayette Avenue.

Once comfortable, he said, "You know, niggers ain't worth shit!" "What's going on?" "My sister promised me the use of her car, everything was set up yesterday and I was just informed from one of her coworkers that she's gone for the day." "Did you try calling her?" "My cell phone batteries are dead."

He needed the car to obtain additional paperwork for his potential bus-driving job with the MTA. He had passed the test and physical but a little more information was needed from somewhere in Prince George's County. They gave him a week to get it in but he was excited about the job and desired to get the material to MTA immediately. He got caught up in the recession two years ago and presently was making a little more than minimum wage.

This guy was told about the importance of me being independent and not relying on anyone unless absolutely necessary. "Sir, this is just a suggestion, look, the Marc train leaves from Penn Station every hour on the hour and the fare is $14.00 roundtrip. You can get off at either New Carrollton or Union Station and connect with Metro to Prince George's County." The man hesitated, thought for a minute, and then said, "Thanks, take me to Penn Station." He was wished all the best after paying the cab fare.

Story #31

Today, our City will be in a complete tizzy, primarily with pedestrians and the traffic in close proximity to the Inner Harbor. The United States' Republicans in Congress will hear President Obama speak at the Marriott Waterfront Hotel. There was a huge display of uniformed police and the upright stanchions were ready but not yet positioned for various detours and blockades.

The cab was stopped for the westbound red light at 25th and Greenmount. There, it was approached by a black man yelling, "Yo, get me to the Mitchell Courthouse as fast as possible. My friend is facing some serious time and the testimony that I'll give today may set him free."

We continued on 25th Street, making a left at St. Paul. Traffic was flowing relatively smooth but was beginning to thicken once we crossed North Avenue. We became bumper to bumper after Biddle Street but still creeping along. My passenger said, "What the fuck is going on man?" "Sir, the President is speaking at a downtown hotel." He said, "Shit, I'm needed in that courthouse, now!"

Once, we had reached St. Paul at Centre Street, there traffic was detoured to the left. Basically, we couldn't move another inch after turning. The man said, "I've got ten minutes before being considered late for court and still there's security. Here's $10.00", he jumped from the cab and hauled-ass down St. Paul Street. Wanting to say, all the best but he was long gone.

The situation just got worst. Traffic came to a complete standstill for all of downtown's east/west traffic. I was told by more than one passenger later in the day that security was extremely tight. Some people had to remain in their buildings and others walked for blocks out of the way just to get directly across the street. People were mad but they were informed weeks in advance about President Obama's visit.

It was an honor and privilege to have the President of the United States come to our City. However, I was damn glad when he left so that the streets of Baltimore could be reopened for the free flow of traffic. There's definitely no money to be made in this business while standing still.

Story#32

The cruise ship was in, the dispatcher flashed on the computer screen that cabs were needed at the Port Covington Terminal. Hey, I was right in the area just letting a fare off at Wal-Mart. Here again, it's a crapshoot because you don't know these people's destination. Laughingly, it could be the terminal's parking lot. Hey, it happens. But, thinking positively I'm looking toward the brighter side - those traveling farther in the State or beyond.

The cab was signaled up to the terminal. There I was met by a couple in their fifties who had lots of luggage. The man finally got into the cab after making sure that all their bags were securely in the trunk. He said that his wife had three suitcases including a hanging travel bag to his one. I just laughed, saying, "That's a woman for you." Their destination was Columbia Maryland. *All right*, saying to myself.

"How was the cruise?" "Oh, don't ask! It was our first and we were treated royally. The service was excellent. It was a seven-day cruise and we had the *BALL* of our lives. It's what my husband and I needed. We definitely found ourselves again after all these years! Didn't we Sweetie?" "Really, that's great Miss, sounds like a story in itself."

"But, you know, on the serious side, you never know what's around the corner! There was this couple aboard. The husband had a heart attack while visiting one of the islands. An ambulance transported him to the island's hospital. The hospital was found to be inadequate, so his wife inquired about airlifting him to Miami for treatment.

"At this point, they found their medical insurance coverage was of no use outside the United States. *Cash or credit card was needed to cover all medical expenses*." She said, "That was heavy, real heavy," and affectionately kissed her man on the cheek. "We didn't take the health insurance offered when booking the cruise but you can bet your sweet-ass after experiencing that we will!"

Story #33

A white woman, say between 35-40 years old was noticed in my side view mirror running towards the cab at the intersection of Pratt and Greene Streets. "Hey, I've been chasing you for a minute, take me to the Hotel Monaco. Do you have change for a $50.00?" "No!" "First, let's stop at the Sunoco filling station down on Russell Street."

She was definitely buzzed from drugs and kept rubbing her eyes intensely. This lady jumped from the cab like a track star at the service station, leaving my door wide open. She returned, still complaining about her eyes and begging for God's help. "This is serious, I'm losing my eye sight or something, take me to Mercy's emergency ward."

All speed limits were exceeded flying down Pratt to Calvert Street. "I don't know what's going on but those fucking drugs ain't worth my eye sight. Mister, I took a hit of coke after leaving the City Morgue. My nerves got the best of me after being questioned by them dumb-assed police and having to identify my man of 10 years." She handed me $10.00 while flying up Calvert Street, saying don't worry about the change, jumped from the cab and ran into the ER.

I saw her a few days later while staged on University Hospital's cabstand. She told me that she had been tripping with a mixture of cocaine and prescription drugs.

Story #34

Baltimore City has hosted cheerleading competitions for years. It was dark and the convention was breaking for the evening. These four hot-tailed well-shaped teenage girls approached at the convention center cabstand. One sticking her head inside the window on the passenger side asking, "Are you available Sir?" "Sure, where to?" "The Tremont Plaza Hotel on St. Paul Street."

They got in, one sitting up front and they immediately started talking about some guy being a *hottie*. One girl in the back said, "I'd French kiss him all day long and who knows what would happen next?" They all agreed that he was definitely buff.

They requested some hip-hop station on the radio. The girl up front scanned and found what they wanted to hear. Stopped in the next lane for the light at Calvert and Lombard Streets was this *tough* looking BMW with aluminum wheels, thin tires and the windows were heavily tinted. *It was clean.* All the cab's windows were down, the girls commented on how *bad* the car was. One even leaned out the window eyeing the vehicle pleasurably.

The driver slowly let his window down, smiled and winked. The girl who leaned out the back window became quite flirtatious with this black dude. He expressed excitement by showing his gold grill and wiggled his tongue at her as the light changed. One girl said, "What have you done," as the guy tailed us to the hotel with his car.

All four became nervous and scared. They let the windows up and asked me to lock the doors. They paid me quickly and haul-assed out the cab and into hotel, never looking back. The gold tooth driver stopped parallel to the cab, looked and just drove away.

Story #35
My strategy was to cruise north on Eutaw Street after leaving Camden Yards. I had noticed that a crowd had formed in front of the Hippodrome Theatre after crossing Baltimore Street. Everyone was looking towards the ground. A young white lady was having an epileptic seizure. Her body was bobbing. The onlookers were just watching, nothing else, nobody was doing a damn thing.

There was a small-framed policewoman on the scene about five feet tall. She appeared to be a rookie. The uniform and equipment were sagging off her body. The first aid training from my cop days kicked in advising someone to place a key or pen in the lady's mouth. This will prevent her from swallowing or biting her tongue in half.

The lady cop said, "You ain't no doctor. Someone could get sued for wrongful advice." "No problem, Officer," I saluted her and just went on about my business.

Story #36

It was Halloween night, the ghosts and goblins were out, I decided to go with the money, and started around 9:30PM. Knowing there would be heavy transportation demands on the menu from Hopkins, Loyola and Towson State Universities. These schools will be rocking and rolling all night long; primarily to and from Fells Point.

Cab 1941 had stopped for the red light at the intersection of Charles and Centre Streets when approached by an Asian man who needed service. His destination was Johns Hopkins Bayview Hospital. He complained that because it's Halloween night cab service is awful.

"What are you talking about Sir?" "My girlfriend, who's a chemist, worked a 12 hour shift at Johns Hopkins Bayview Hospital, has been calling for the last two hours for a cab. The dispatcher keeps saying one's on the way when she returns the call requesting an estimated time of arrival."

"Sir, it's understood what you're saying." Because it is Halloween Night, the majority of cabs are strategically staging around various colleges dorms in the City and the rest are probably sitting up at Penn Station. These situations definitely hamper individuals who call for service.

"Driver, you think, we can make this a round trip." "Sure, no problem", knowing it will yield at least $30.00. "Man, you're a good dude; your girlfriend's got to be most grateful. I sincerely hope that she'll be appeasing this evening for your concerns and treats you like a king." He said, "Yeah, yeah, yeah, I hope so too!"

He called, telling her that we were five minutes away. She was waiting at Bayview's red awning with a smile on her face as we approached. They kissed and had a pleasant conversation en route back to Park Avenue and Centre Street. He gave me $40.00 on a $30.00 fare, which was appreciated. This was an excellent start for the evening.

Story #37
Halloween came right this particular year, Saturday night and the town was jumping, all hot spots were crowded. Got a good start, had made well over my goal much earlier than expected. The freaks were definitely out! There were many creative and elaborate costumes - some were quite unusual. The money was flowing heavily within the boundaries of Federal Hill, the Inner Harbor, Fells Point and Canton. It was a cab driver's dream. All you wanted to do was stay in the zone until the bottom burned out!

While traveling west on Fort Avenue approaching Webster Street, a white man about 25 years old flagged. He asked if credit cards were accepted and needed transportation well beyond Interstate #83. He then requested me to wait while he informed his brother about his plan. Once seated comfortably in the cab, he informed me that he works 10 to 15 hours a day and that he was just tired. "What do you do, where do you work?" "I'm an information technology technician for a major television network."

He had always been interested in computers and gained much experience from radio stations as a teenager, having worked at five stations. "So, you are telling me that you have no formal

training and all your knowledge was on the job training."
"Yes, my experiences were great and have made excellent
money for a man of my age. But the stress is tremendous. You
would not believe how costly it can be because of dead time.
The world can be experiencing its worst disaster and you are
expected to keep radio/television stations up. They don't care
about acts of God or any other interference."

He said that he has been to the top of the tower on Television
Hill twice. "I know you don't walk to the top of that thing."
"No, there's an elevator in a section of the tower, which really
isn't that safe. You walk, then take an elevator almost to the
top. Aside from the height and a magnificent view, it is
extremely dangerous up there! The intensity from the lights
causes your blood to boil. The elevator is known to drop about
15 stories when descending and the emergency brake switch
cannot be pulled. Eventually, it resumes at a regular
descending pace." That's like real, real HEAVY!

We took exit #12 off I-83 and went west on Old Court Road
for about a mile, driving up a dark secluded private road with
deer jumping all over the place, finally stopping at this shack
for a house. The fare was $45.00. His credit card was
presented for payment, telling me to take $75.00. Being
flabbergasted, he could not have been thanked enough! This
was one interesting fare!

Story #38
Driving becomes tiring, at times, you need to stop, relax and
position your vehicle in a place that is convenient for taxicab
service. The Gallery Mall at Calvert and Pratt Streets was my
choice. The cab was not even completely parked before being
approached by tourists who later shared that they were New
Yorkers.

They inquired about the Great Blacks in Wax Museum. I told them "It's in an old firehouse uptown about 2 ½ miles from here in East Baltimore, like a $10.00 to $12.00 cab ride." "Please, take us there." "No problem, Sir." "You know, at times cab service can be difficult in that section of the City. Here's my calling card, try calling 15 minutes ahead for pickup."

They called about two hours later, requesting to be picked up from Walgreens Drugstore located at North Avenue and Harford Road directly across from one of Baltimore's busiest District Courts.

They were asked about their opinion of the museum. His wife said, "It's so damn depressing why we haven't advanced any further as a people. To actually see real life-like figures of our ancestors - knowing what they fought for and some even lost their lives for and where we are today - is unbelievable! The equal opportunities they dreamed of, what they wanted and accomplished for Negroes coloreds, Blacks and African Americans - then to see and realize the postures and positions of many in today's society is absolutely unreal. Just what has happened to our people! Cab driver, I need a drink to try and digest all of this!" "Miss, it's totally understood."

Story #39
Morgan State University's Harper House called for a cab. This dorm is located on the north side of the campus. There the cab was approached by two19 year old students who were going out for the night. My goodness, these young ladies were dressed to kill! The Velvet Rope in downtown Baltimore was their destination.

My tongue slipped while heading downtown saying "Didn't the police commissioner padlock that nightclub for being a public nuisance?" That had to be a Freudian slip, most definitely. They called by cell phone, the answering service indicated the club is only open Thursday thru Saturday.

We were south on St. Paul approaching Penn Station. There, they decided to try the Haven Lounge in Northwood Shopping Center. So, we headed back uptown. Only to find the Haven's doorman was carding, thought to myself, Morgan must not have an illegal ID specialist on campus.

"Sir, we're going somewhere but first take us to the student center on campus." They were told that Club One and Bourbon Street were open and both cater to 18 year olds in downtown Baltimore. This information was taken for face value only to find them also closed. "Just take us back to campus."

Their fare was $31.00 at this point and they had accomplished nothing. We were still downtown, not wanting to drain these students of their little money, a deal was made for the entire trip for $35.00.

You know, this is absolutely ridiculous. Morgan State University has approximately 8,000 students and there is no place in the immediate area that caters to these college students. Not even Northwood Shopping Center, which is directly across the street. That school has been at its present location since the 1930's, this was during the Jim Crow era.

The majority of the immediate neighborhoods that surrounded the University then were white and segregated. I remembered vividly Morgan's students being incarcerated for participating in the integration of the Northwood Theatre in Northwood Shopping Center. Also, when the immediate neighborhoods became integrated, Blacks were steered to purchase homes on streets anywhere off Loch Raven Boulevard, but not on Loch

Raven itself. Like, who makes these decisions, where do they originate?

It's believed that Northwood Shopping Center could have been the jewel for African Americans in this City, definitely being an economic engine, drawing students, their friends, relatives and patrons from the school, many surrounding neighborhoods and quite possibly African Americans throughout the country. Baltimore is 65% African American in population and Northwood Shopping Center could have been a major venue equivalent to Baltimore's Inner Harbor.

Morgan State University definitely needs a hotel in close proximity for its VIP's and people it draws for various activities scheduled throughout the school year. The Hecht Company building in Northwood Shopping Center, which was vacant for over 20 years, certainly could have served that purpose. There is adequate parking, approximately 15 storefronts in this strip mall and a blocked off movie theatre. Presently, many of the stores there are sub-standard and not an asset to the University or the neighborhood.

If done correctly, this could have been a great opportunity for many first class black-owned businesses in this African American Community, with restaurants presenting a fine dining atmosphere, cafe, swanky nightclub with a jazz club, bookstore, electronics and cell phone outlet, banking, jewelry store, game room and more.

Where were the African American developers and entrepreneurs; did any of them ever have a vision (present or beyond) to capitalize off Morgan State University's market and its immediate neighborhoods after the area became totally integrated? It's to my understanding that a PowerPoint presentation concerning the matter was discussed but to no avail.

Once again, the Reisterstown Road corridor from Haywood Avenue to the City line looks promising as an African American commercial, financial and cultural arts district - especially since the Department of Motor Vehicles recently relocated across from the five Mile House Bar and Restaurant. We'll see!

Think about this, every ethnic group in Baltimore has a proud business section, such as the Italians have Little Italy, the Jewish have Upper Park Heights and the Latinos have what is referred to as their own little paradise!

Story #40

Cab 1914 bid on a computerized call in the Lake Roland section of the City. A well-dressed white gentleman around 45 years old with luggage in tow signaled while I was turning onto a side street south of the intersection of Lake and Roland Avenues. "Driver, are you going to *such and such address*?" "Yes sir."

"It must be quite busy down there," he said, after being seated and baggage secured. "No Sir, not in the least." "Actually, I'm pissed; I've been calling the Cab Company continuously for the last hour and a half when you saw me. I have walked three blocks from my house and need to get to Penn Station immediately!" Services are absolutely terrible since the Cab Company was sold to a company overseas. This was one of Baltimore's carte blanche companies.

His final statement at Penn Station was that "losing the public's confidence can be highly detrimental to the company's existence." He added, "From my experiences when small companies are acquired by out-of-state corporations, the results are not always best for the consumer." "Understood, Sir!"

Story #41

A black man about 45 years old, flagged at Fayette and Highland Streets by the Farm Store; he took a final hale from his cigarette before entering the cab. "Good evening Sir, take me to the 8600 block Eastern Avenue. I'd appreciate you taking Lombard Street's extension that runs behind Johns Hopkins Bayview Hospital. Cabbie, this is my day off, Man, I'm just tired, but this overtime money is definitely needed."

I'm thinking to myself, what business is located in the 8600 block of Eastern Avenue. It finally surfaced. "You work at the waste treatment plant, don't you?" "Yes!"

His response led me to asking questions about the processing of human shit before it is released into Back River. There are various filtration substations around the City before it gets to Eastern Avenue. The waste is strained, removing all the large objects and paper. Then, it is boiled at a very high temperature that removes the bacteria.

The smells that are encountered on Eastern Avenue are the processing chemicals and not the waste itself. Inspectors are there at all times checking for any infractions of waste treatment processing.

He said, "We're required to have physicals every 6 months checking for various bacteria that cause diseases. An employee once fell into this huge shit tank, he survived but man was he a mess for a good while. He had all types of problems stemming from ammonia burns over 90 percent of his body. After all that, you know, he refused to take a buy-out and returned to the job once recovered." Ain't that some shit!

Story #42

An African American woman about 50 years old standing in front of the Northeast Market on East Monument Street signaled. "Good Afternoon Sir, I'd like to go to 2400 block West Lafayette Avenue in West Baltimore. This certainly is a clean cab." "Thank you Miss, that's my old neighborhood, we lived on Calverton Heights Avenue, had great times there. We were among the first black families on the block."

She started talking about City Hall's corruption. How Mayor Sheila Dixon has brought shame and disgrace to our City nationally. Next week cannot come fast enough for her removal from office. "I sincerely hope that Councilwoman Stephanie Rawlings-Blake does an admirable job as mayor for the remainder of the term. Baltimore's African American race is devastated!" I said, "Oh, I don't know about that. As a cab driver, I've actually seen much accomplished under Sheila's administration."

She said, "You know, greed, power and corruption seem to have penetrated many facets of our society. I was totally loyal to my church, which is located in East Baltimore, and maintained a very good position within. But, circumstances have forced me to leave the church as of last year." "Why so?"

"My husband and I were planning our daughter's wedding. She was to be married in the family's church. They wanted $1800 for use of the facility, which includes the pastor's fee and a $300 rehearsal fee, all up front. I was absolutely appalled regarding the rehearsal fee, especially after being affiliated with the church for 25 years."

"Miss, I'm not a real church person but as a business person knowing that expenses are involved, but still, that sounds to be a bit absurd. I bet there's an ATM machine in the church vestibule." "There is!"

Story #43
The dispatcher pleaded with the drivers over the computer to take a taxi access job in the vicinity of The Alameda Circle in Northeast Baltimore. The party was called out upon my arrival. Someone acknowledged by flicking the front porch light. Moments later, this dude hurriedly pushing someone in a wheelchair came from around the corner saying the cab's for them. I really did not feel up to dealing with no wheelchair person this time of night. Their character and personal hygiene or lack of is evident in the chair. Gloves are used when handling.

The front seat was needed because of the man's disability. "You know, this is a roundtrip to York and Glenwood, don't you." "No, I didn't, but since you're a taxi access passenger, your return trip will be cash." "No problem." They started talking in some type of code when discussing how much money is needed, knowing their mission is for drugs.

The area in question is known for heavy drug trafficking. Many neighborhoods in this City have drug hotspots. Some are even operational 24 hours a day with lookouts strategically stationed to send signals when 5-0 is approaching. Junkies hustle hard in order to maintain their own habit. Their drug stashes are in close proximity but for the most part never found on them. It is obvious that the war on drugs has failed in this town despite law enforcements high tech equipment and surveillances. Without a doubt, drugs have played a significant role in the demise of many Baltimore City neighborhoods.

The man seated up front said, "Here's all the money that I have." Get what you can! There were lots of people just standing around when he got out the cab. It was quite obvious from observing that he could not find his connection. So, he went into the bar, stayed a minute and came out with some dude. They went down Glenwood Avenue and disappeared behind the Chinese carryout joint. He returned to the cab moments later and said, "Let's go."

We traveled south on York and across Cold Spring Lane en route back to The Alameda Circle. "You know, I could be the police," I basically know that my man in the back is dirty as shit. Police do disguise as cabbies and patrol many hot spots in the City. "Ah-h-h Man, you too goddamn old to be the police." "Hey, beware, you never know." Many cops especially these rookies strive on any type of a drug case. Wheelchair bound or not means absolutely nothing; your black ass will go to jail with the rest of them.

Story #44
I had just dropped off my passengers at Baltimore and Highland who had been picked up from Perkins, a public housing project. While en route to Hopkins' taxicab stand, driving westbound on Fayette Street approaching Lakewood, cars were slowing because a black man about 30 years old, with a young baby in his arms and a 3 years old boy barely keeping up, was dancing around the traffic in the middle of the street.

The man was hysterical, crying, speech slurred and had tears and snot streaming down his face. Motorists slowed, rubber necking, but just kept on driving. The man was at the cab's window holding this limp child. "What's going on?" He was extremely excited but after looking at the child and realizing that he appeared not to be breathing I yelled, "Get in!" We traveled fast going through three red lights towards Hopkins' ER. Again, the man was asked what happened. "How the FUCK do I know, just get me to goddamn hospital ASAP."

My teeth were gritted, in order to hold back my words! "Mister is the child breathing?" "I don't know." He was really screaming, hollering and acting extremely desperate at this point. I told him to lay the child down on the backseat, blow intervals of air into his mouth and apply pressure to the chest. While this was being done he repeatedly said, "Just get me to the fucking hospital!"

Mind you, it was about 5PM during rush hour traffic and Fayette Street was jammed. The traffic signal at Wolfe was red, passengers were boarding an MTA Bus at the corner and the cab was four car lengths back in the westbound outside lane. He screamed at me, "Go around the goddamn cars!" The cab was angled over into the eastbound lane. "Mister, I just can't do it." "Why?" Wolfe Street is one way south, the bus was blocking my view, in addition to being four cars back from the light, couldn't do it, can't do it, won't do it. We could have very easily been involved in a serious head on collision. After saying that, moments later a car came speeding around the corner.

At wits end, he jumped from the cab running, child in arms and the 3 years boy following; leaving my rear right door wide open. This wild, ignorant acting, frantic and scared man was doing what he knew to save his child. By speeding up and jamming on the brakes after the light changed the door was swung shut. The intersection of Wolfe and Fayette Streets is the southern boundary of the Hopkins Complex. The Hopkins Hospitals Harriett Lane Children's Center is located at the 200 N. Wolfe.

The traffic light caught me at Fayette and Broadway. While stopped, a white lady in the other lane said that she was behind me and saw everything. She then asked, was he breathing? "I don't know Miss, but I certainly hope so." As the light was changing, she said, "That was very nice what you did!" "Thank you, Miss."

Hopkins called for cabs at the Wolfe Street entrance. The fare's destination was Admiral Fell's Inn. The most direct route was south on Wolfe Street. Basically, traffic was at a standstill because an ambulance was blocking the lane in front on Harriet Lane Children's Center, assuming it was there for the child. The ambulance was empty when we passed with its lights flashing and doors wide open.

My curiosity was at an all time high, so I immediately responded back to Harriett Lane after dropping off the fare. After telling my side of the story, the receptionist told me the boy was okay and that he was out of danger. His medical problem could not be revealed because of patient confidentiality. He was taken to Hopkins ER for children. I sighed with relief and was thankful that he was alive. Hey, hats off to the father!

Story #45
The cab was literally running on fumes, I pulled into the Exxon Station located at Greene and Mulberry Streets. A casually dressed black woman about 40 years old ran across the street from the Social Security Building telling me that she had a family emergency, stole away from her job and needs to get back there ASAP! "I'm going to get me a soda while you gas up." "No problem, Miss."

This wait was longer than usual. The horn was blown with no response. I got out the cab after an additional five minutes had lapsed, peeked through the service station window and observed the woman in the lottery line behind five people with a list in hand. There appeared to be mixed priorities here, so "Adios."

The Maryland State Lottery is huge and yields an awful lot of money. It cuts across all cultures in the City and discriminates against none. Some individuals spend lots of money on the daily lottery games. I have often wondered what is the percentage for Baltimore City and where is the money earmarked. The numbers game was big business in Baltimore City's African American community prior to becoming legal in Maryland.

Story #46

Radio dispatched me to the east parking lot of Baltimore City College High School (City) off The Alameda. It was known as the Castle on the Hill when I attended. Responding to this particular call definitely brought back memories. All being said, sitting here is freaking me out!

Finally, a young white woman approached the cab. She was casually dressed, environmentalist-style, carrying a backpack with the obligatory water bottle attached. At first, she was mistaken for a student but after refocusing, I realized her to be a young adult about 24 years old. Her destination was BWI Airport.

Our conversation revealed that she had been teaching at City College for two years. "Miss, I attended this school many years ago. Its standards were very high. Then, it was an all male school and the majority of the student population was Jewish." "I've heard," she said. "During those years, students had lots of school freedom. You could actually leave the campus, as long as you were on time for the next scheduled class. The year's highlight was the City/Poly football game played on Thanksgiving Day at Memorial Stadium. The stadium was located directly across 33rd Street from the school. Does the school still have fairly liberal freedom for the students?"

"No! There are armed, uniformed police at all Baltimore City middle and high schools now. This school is co-ed and has gone through various principals, primarily because Baltimore City Public Schools' initiatives."

"If, I remember correctly, City was a citywide enrichment school when it reopened. The students had to be tested for admittance. They had to be on grade level or excelled in English, mathematics and science in addition to having an interview." "Well, I teach Algebra and most of my students are passing, however there is a small percentage in my class who can't find the least common denominator of a fraction." "Really," I said. "Yes, there are always some who have difficulties."

"I know some students have to give you an absolute fit discipline wise being so young and white." "Sir, tears have been withheld until I'm able to find privacy to cry." "Since City is a citywide school, can't the troublemakers be diverted back to their zoned school?" "I really don't know. Our interim principal is doing an excellent job keeping City on target. I love to teach, this has been my passion since elementary school."

"Do you have friends in other school jurisdictions?" "Yes, Baltimore and Howard counties. The majority of their students are on grade level, classrooms much smaller, the schools are adequately supplied and there is good parent participation. Their challenges are not as stressful by any stretch of the imagination that I have encountered. Well, I'm going to visit my parents and friends in San Francisco for the weekend."

"So, where do you live in the City?" "Three other teachers and I share a house in Upton located in West Baltimore. Do you know of the neighborhood?" "Yes, I know where it is. You live there!" This area is deep in the heart of West Baltimore's ghettos. "Have you had a chance to visit the various attractions around the City?" "I've been to the Harbor and Fells Point but I rather prefer sitting on the stoops talking with my neighbors."

As we approached BWI Airport, I admired this young lady from San Francisco but I was puzzled and really could not figure her mission, was it for the experience, data for book or just a change from the norm or what. One thing for sure, whatever the reason she will always have options!

After paying the cab fare, she expressed how she enjoyed the ride and conversation. I said, "You know, lately I've been giving the United States Peace Corps a lot of thought. There's really no age limitations." She said, "From my point of view I definitely encourage you to try it. That sounds wonderful." Then we laughed, "Have a good flight...City Forever!"

Story #47
Cab 1914 accepted the call to the President's Office of the University of Maryland on Arch Street. This building has 14 stories, ten of which are for parking and the top three for offices. It is located directly across from the Social Security building on Saratoga Street. You talk about security.

I was met there by a gentleman who was professional looking. His request was UMBC in Baltimore County. He commented on the Ravens' as we passed the stadium on Russell Street, asking "Who's gonna win this Thanksgiving classic between the two Harbaugh brothers who coach opposing teams?" "My money's on John Harbaugh, all the way. There has to be a tremendous amount of team pressure from both the Ravens and the 49ers." "What's the parents' position on this classic?" "I don't know but they have to be extremely proud! We always are when our children make significant accomplishments."

He talked of being tenured for years as a `professor at UMBC. "The school has changed all for the good since Dr. Freeman Harbowski became President. He has done a magnificent job academically especially in the studies of math and the science. We're definitely on the move." "Yes, I see that was a quality piece that *60 Minutes* did on the University and Dr. Harbowski. Hey, that's real good press, nationally and prime time TV too. The Polish origin of his name was found to be quite interesting as an African American."

"Dr. Harbowski expressed such enthusiasm about various accomplishments the students have made at UMBC. He talked of them learning to attack problems or situations as a group, which to me is dynamic, and of their strive for excellence in preparing for this global society. I was thoroughly impressed with the incoming freshman class's lack of attrition come graduation some four years later. He's telling us what most of us have heard all our entire lives that education will definitely transform your life."

"Well sir, we're in trouble from what's seen through this windshield. The influx of foreigners in the City's universities and work force is serious and they are serious. Not being funny, but they run all the mom and pop businesses and know the system. The question is often asked - who's the foreigner here!"

Story #48

An African approached the cab and asked was I working while parked and reading the newspaper at the intersection of Greene and Baltimore Streets. "Yes Sir." "How much to Eastern Avenue and I-95?" "I'd say between twenty and twenty-five dollars. That's a rough estimate."

"What do you normally pay?" "I'd say about $15.00." "Mister, no way, that's clear across town on the other side on Bayview Hospital." "True, but its nowhere near that price when traveling through the tunnel." "Hey, the tunnel fee is $3.00." "Don't worry about that, I'll take care of it." Saying to myself - *Which is customary*. It's a straight shot, why not. Although, he's really getting over big time!

We discussed American politics once on the interstate. I was impressed! He knew his stuff. "What's your background?" "I teach at one of the City's universities and have a doctorate degree from Hopkins." "You have what?" He repeated it. "I'm on a tight budget." "No shit, we all live on budgets." This behavior is typical of some regardless of their economic status. They always want a deal, man or woman! He gave me a $50 bill to pay the tariff at the toll plaza. Really, this shit is just unbelievable; it is insulting, rude and arrogant!

"Mister, I'm gonna tell you something. We made a deal and that's that. But your bullshit is unacceptable. It's obvious that you must get tremendous pleasures from hustling people."

He said no more, gave me what we agreed on after I returned his change from the $50 bill and said thanks at his destination. I showed my disgust by saying absolutely nothing, displaying an angry look. You can't imagine how pissed I was. The accelerator was stomped to the floor getting back into the lane of traffic.

Story #49
Booked in the East Monument Street taxi zone and was immediately dispatched to the 500 block North Streeper; someone acknowledged by saying they would be right out. Moments later, two ladies stepped from a row house; the younger one dragging a backpack on wheels as the other lady with a cane was having difficulty walking. They hugged, kissed and said goodbye, the younger lady said, "Love you Mama" as she returned to the house. The lady appeared beat own from the years but quite possibly could be younger then what she looked, if you know what is meant.

The computer indicated her destination being Greyhound Bus in downtown Baltimore. She said, "I'm through with Greyhound since Bolt Bus came into existence." I told her that Bolt Bus is owned and operated by Greyhound and the reason it came about was because the Chinese operated buses at much cheaper roundtrip rates from Washington, D.C. to Boston than the commercial bus lines. The fare from Baltimore to New York City is $20.00 one way and $35.00 roundtrip. The kicker being one has to wait curbside at an unprotected designated bus stop for its arrival. But, the buses are new with comfortable seating and equipped with Wi-Fi. That must be worth the inconvenience because the curbside lines are becoming longer and longer daily.

Anyway, the computer had her destination wrong, "Take me to the Bolt Bus stop in the1600 block St. Paul Street." The lady requested me to stop somewhere en route for cigarettes. We stopped at the Sunoco Gas Station located Orleans and Washington Streets. It took awhile for her to get out the cab to make the purchase. Once returning, she asked, "Will the fare be more than $10.00?" "Miss, this is a metered cab, really don't know. The fare should run between $10.00 to $12.00 dollars depending upon the traffic."

In the 1600 block North Charles the Bolt Bus was seen in clear view across the open-air parking lot on St. Paul Street with passengers boarding. The cab was angled in front the bus blocking its departure. The meter read $12.00, which included a dollar for the service call. She handed me a ten-dollar bill saying, "That's all I got Mister." "The fare is $12.00, Miss, what do you mean that's all you got?"

"You expect me to believe that you're going to New York City and have no money." "I don't Mister. Well, you can go back to the house and get the two dollars from my daughter." "The nerve of you Miss, to take a portion of your taxi fare to purchase cigarettes, then tell me that you're short. How dare you, my mind tells me to lock these damn doors and return your ass to Streeper Street. You don't need to be smoking anyway. But, instead, you enjoy your ride to New York City and please remember the cab driver that you cut short to buy those cancer sticks for your enjoyment."

Story #50
My fares' destination was the Delta Terminal at BWI. The lady who appeared to be desperately in need of transportation approached the cab as my passenger's luggage was being retrieved from the trunk. She needed to get to the Russian Consulate in Washington, D.C. ASAP in 30 minutes. Which is highly impossible!

We might get to the Washington D.C. line in the allotted time but not clear across town on the other side of Dupont Circle during the evening rush hour where I guess this consulate is located. She needed transportation immediately, running behind schedule and having no other alternative. Like, why not, if not me then the next available cab.

68

Anyway, my primary objective was to get this lady in the cab and away from this airport before being approached by the Maryland Transportation Police. The penalties are rough. They can be far more severe then this $100 ride to D.C. But I needed and wanted the money. Plus, the break was appreciated.

Honestly, I really did not know where she was going but had a general idea. Most of the embassies are either located on Massachusetts Avenue NW or in close proximity. The consulate was in the 2600 block Tunlaw Road NW. A fellow cabbie was contacted and advised Tunlaw Road was around the U.S. Observatory Circle. My passenger called a Russian friend who also revealed this place was in the vicinity of Massachusetts and Wisconsin Avenues.

We were both relieved; especially me - she hired my services believing that I was knowledgeable of the destination. Actually, I'm still not sure of the exact location of this street. The cab company's GPS is limited with a range about 30 miles from Baltimore's Inner Harbor. My intentions were to ask a D.C. cabbie when in the vicinity.

My passenger was going to the Russian Consulate to renew her visa. The appointment was 4:00 PM sharp and if late, a fine would be imposed. She was supposed to have been picked up by a friend of her husband's six hours ago. "Why didn't you consult with your husband about other arrangements after three hours had passed?" "He just insisted that I wait."

It was suggested that she call the Consulate to explain the situation. The call was made; she finally talked with someone with authority after being transferred around for 15 minutes. The call was definitely a stress reliever.

"My husband caused all this shit! He insisted with his controlling personality that I wait for his friend." She said, "I'm capable, knowledgeable and resourceful enough to find my own way. He paid for my travel to America and thinks that he owns me. We married soon after my arrival. This is my first time away from Memphis, Tennessee and I've been living in the states for five years. My husband wants a child but I don't want his baby. Lately, I've been considering separating and getting divorced."

Well, it figures, no left turn from Massachusetts onto Wisconsin Avenue; made the turn anyway after looking around and observing no cop cars or traffic light camera. I inquired at the Sunoco gas station about three blocks down Wisconsin Avenue about the Russian Consulate on Tunlaw Road. The attendant pointed to the building and said the street's one block over. She paid the fare and thanked me for getting her there promptly. I waited until she was securely on the compound. Now, this fare definitely was the foresight of an aggressive cab driver not letting that money escape!

Story #51
The cab was flagged for service by two Mexican men while returning downtown from the Baltimore National Pike. They were standing in the bus stop adjacent to West Baltimore's Amtrak Station on Mulberry Street. "Can you take me," pointing to himself and friend, "to Broadway's 7-11 Store?" "Yes."

After being seated, they talked in a very fast tongue between each other. I have transported a fair number of Latinos around Baltimore and know from experience that many are as overlooked as are Blacks in this city for cab ridership. To add to their comfort, 107.9 FM, a Spanish radio station was tuned.

They smiled after realizing what they were hearing. One said, "You like a Spanish music?" "Si..."

The fare was $9.00. "Here's a twenty." I gave them a five-dollar bill and six ones. They gave me the $5.00 bill back and smiled showing their gratitude. I said, "Gracias, adios amigos."

Story #52

Responded to a call for service while cruising north on Ellwood from Preston. The front door of the house was opened to acknowledge after blowing the cab's horn. Moments later this cute, 5'7" tall brown-skinned young lady with wide hips wearing a tight pair of designer jeans came from the walkway and entered the vehicle on my blind side.

Talking in a low sweet voice with what appeared to be a New York accent, she said, "Good evening Sir, would you take me to the hotel on Pulaski Highway. But first, I need to wire some money; would you happen to know of a Western Union Office in the neighborhood?" "No, not really, but money grams can be sent from CVS drugstore. There's one located at Belair and Erdman." "Take me there, please."

She then could be heard counting money and said, "Shit, that bastard could have given me a better tip then this." It took her about 15 minutes in CVS to transact business. We traveled north on Belair Road en route to the hotel. Her phone rang about midway; she answered and said, "What's up dude." Obviously, it was a john seeking sex from the overheard conversation. He asked, "What's your price?" She replied, "$80.00 for a quickie and $100.00 for a half hour." The quickie must be head.

71

He hesitated. Then she said, "Let me know when you're ready. I'm still working out the same place." That conversation ended. The fare was paid and a $10.00 tip was given. She was thanked, really thanked, and carefully observed when leaving the cab and disappearing within the hotel's lobby. Saying to myself and smiling, "I'd love to have accommodated!"

Story #53

You know, there's nothing more annoying when riding empty than hearing a cell phone ring or vibrate on the backseat. Invariably, you know what comes next after answering the phone. *Driver, will you bring me my phone*? My passengers are given an option for the most part. Their property can be picked up from the cab company's lost and found the following day unless there's a reward involved.

Hating to be a hard ass, but time lost is definitely money! It is not my fault that they failed to make that final check before closing the cab's door. I can't be responsible for their negligence! There again, I do realize the importance of their telephone. Consequently, a monetary value has to be placed on the immediate return of their property. That is determined by time required from my location to theirs.

My cab was hailed in the 400 East Baltimore Street, otherwise known as the Block or Baltimore's red light district. The fare handed me a ringing cell phone found on the backseat while entering the cab. I said to myself, *Shit*! The person offered a reward and told me to call this number when in front of the nursing home opposite St. Agnes Hospital. "Sir, I'll be there within an hour."

He was called out after arriving. Moments later, he and this lady came out the nursing home. He thanked me for being so prompt, saying, "Its content is of great value." "Do you have what we discussed?" "No, I ain't got no money but I need my phone." Saying, "Well Mister," after sliding the phone back into my pocket, "it'll be at the cab company around 12 noon tomorrow."

You know, we damn near came to blows over this phone shit until the lady came between us and paid the money. This man was offered an option! The nerve of that bastard going back on his word like that after having me drive this distance from downtown Baltimore.

Story #54

It was getting late and I was becoming tired from a grueling day's work. My money wasn't right so I needed to keep on plugging. Primarily, business has been absolutely terrible during this recession. Booked into Hopkins' zone on my computer and was immediately given a charge account job. Well, Lo and behold when pulling into the main entrance of the hospital's driveway I noticed a real heavy black lady in an oversized wheelchair accompanied by a nurse and hospital guard with an overloaded cart of personal belongings. Saying to myself after glazing over to my computer that it's a good trip, paying about $30.00 but really don't feel up to this shit.

The trunk was popped while approaching. "What's going on?" I asked when exiting the cab and laughing to the nurse, "And what department are you from?" "Psych department, she's being released after a three month stay." It literally took 15 minutes in getting this lady's personal things including a wheelchair and stationary chair that needed placing on the front seat of the cab upside down.

The lady was heavy; it took all her concentration and effort for the transfer from the wheelchair to the cab. She lived in the Forest Park section of town around Belle and Garrison

Boulevard. We became engaged in good conversation, telling me that she suffers from a bipolar disorder and has to be institutionalized periodically in addition to being on dialysis. Those are two tough illnesses. She was a talker, appeared *kinda* happy to be away from Hopkins and sang along with the tunes on the radio while riding up I-83.

Her daughter was called from my cellular phone, "Hi, this is the cab driver; we'll be in front of your door in five minutes." Just as the conversation ended, an alert from my computer advised me to contact dispatch ASAP. They told me to return to the hospital immediately, revealing that the patient had someone else's medication. Saying, "Shit, we're at the lady's house." I decided to unload her personal belongings before returning to the hospital. Of course, the house sat back from the street with steep steps leading to the porch. The daughter took her time getting to the door and was of little assistance. She was informed about the call from Hopkins.

On the way back down to Hopkins, the lady said that she had to pee while in the vicinity of Cold Spring Lane and Reisterstown Road. "Miss, please don't pee on yourself in my cab." Mind you, we're about five miles from the hospital. She said, "I'll try not to Mister." The tone of my voice got loud, "What do you mean by that?" "Just, what I said. Mister, really, I got to pee." I immediately make a right turn onto Greenspring Ave and the first right at Edgehurst, stopping midway of the block. The street is small, woody, curvy and dark. Turning to the lady saying, "This is it, do what you have to do." Turning my head around quickly - having no desire to peek. You could hear the struggle in her getting those pants down over that huge ass. The rear right door was opened as the woman attempted to clear the car while peeing. "That was such a relief, thank you, thank you, Mister." Saying, "Indeed, thank you lady for not pissing in my cab."

Her pants were three quarters of the way up when turning into the hospital's driveway. The guard said that he had the medicine and told her to stay in the cab. He looked down at her with pants almost up, laughed not knowing what was going on as she explained her circumstances. Once again, back up I-83 to this lady's residence. What a fare, it was well worth the money earned which by the way far exceeded thirty dollars.

Story #55

My high school's class reunion was recently celebrated. Man, was it a blast! The class graduated in 1963 and this is my first ever to attend. There were those that I had not seen since we graduated. Actually, with the use of our class yearbook we were comparing ourselves from then to now. My God, how some of us have changed drastically! We just looked at each other and laughed. However, one classmate said, "Hey, but we're *here*!"

There are those that did extremely well for themselves while others survived moderately, like me. Some went the college route, others became entrepreneurs but the majority appeared to be associated with a structured work environment. Many were grandparents and some even had great grands. All in all, it was a great event. Also, it enabled me to promote my transportation and photography businesses.

One of my classmates called a week later needing transportation to Annapolis, ASAP. He said, "Pick me up at the Legg Mason Building on International Drive in East Harbor." Once onboard and after he made some business calls, we talked about the enjoyable time had at our class reunion. It brought back so many memories of our high school days.

He revealed that he's made good money over the years selling insurances. The business has been good. "I now have the opportunity to close the biggest account ever in Annapolis and my car fails at the 12th hour. Your service is a lifesaver..." "Thanks!"

The subject of our conversation changed while driving down Interstate #97. He talked about his summer beach home that he has adored for 30 years. "It's just outside of Annapolis on the Chesapeake Bay. That atmosphere relieves my stresses momentarily. It's definitely relaxing and invigorating."

"So, does this community have a name?" "Yes, it's called Highland Beach. Frederick Douglass' Summer Home is located down the street from my house. It is now a National Museum. There're three beaches along that strip of the Chesapeake Bay known as Highland Beach, Oyster Harbor and Arundel on The Bay. These communities were once exclusively owned by African Americans up until 30 years ago." Gentrification is here as well!

"Many children of the original owners never had any great interest in the family beach homes. Some were raised in more sterile suburban environments like Columbia, Maryland. Everything in their lives was relatively new including the swimming clubs and area pools. They would rather stay home and go to the development's recreational facility then spend their weekend on the Chesapeake Bay. Some referred to the beach as the country.

"So consequently, the original owners have grown old and died off. The properties needed repairs, property taxes were due and then there are those who just had no interest. Eventually, these properties were sold for much less then market value. Hey, it's believed they've missed the boat somewhere - land certainly has value over money. Major wars are fought over land!

"Whites know the value of waterfront properties, desiring this location between Annapolis and Washington D.C. and won't hesitate at the opportunities when purchases become available. Many have become year around residents. Some have rebuilt after demolishing existing buildings. It's unreal, they change the rules and regulations, properties are reassessed which contributes to tremendous tax increases. There is nothing that can be done where there's no interest. Whatever is just sold to those with the knowledge and who can afford to purchase.

"Look at Washington D.C.; it was once known as *Chocolate City*. Recently, a report revealed that D.C. is over 50% white and growing. It's all about *money. They* make it, *they* got it and we do not. We'll sell out and move on. Soon, we're gonna be locked out, if we aren't already! Our purposes in the big cities will be work related only."

"Hey, the same thing is happening here in Baltimore. There are many gated high-rise communities downtown around University Hospital. East and southeast sections of this City have transformed right in front of us and many do not even realize it. There is rebirth to these neighborhoods. Some neighborhoods are like a maze, consisting of one-way streets only, 45 degree angle parking and only a few streets to exit. They have become more residential and neighborhood friendly with areas of dining, entertainment and recreational facilities within walking distance."

"It's a ripple effect, slowly but surely whatever the trend is and the majority wants will be obtained by the power of the *almighty dollar and the politicians who are persuaded to make and change laws to their advantage.* It's a win-win situation for *them*, period! Gentrification is a national epidemic for those who can afford it. Basically, it seems like all we're able to do is watch this transformation in progress. *So where does that leave us, the minority? I really don't know!*

"Anyway, this was a good talk. My business meeting is at a secluded restaurant on West Street. You know, that Highland Summer Beach Home was my dream." *We're definitely under attack from all angles and many don't have a clue."*

Story #56

The cab was parked in a no parking zone at 33rd and St. Paul. Hopefully, the parking ticket person is not in the neighborhood. My granddaughter had given me a gift card to Subway for Father's Day. This particular store is conveniently located, ideal for an easy fare after lunch and has outside tables.

A white individual approached and asked for a quarter while I was eating outside and relaxing. "No." He then took the vacant seat adjacent to my table. This homeless man was smoking what appeared to be a stumped cigarette and basically seen observing people as they walked by on St. Paul Street. The eye candy was blossoming this beautiful spring day, really.

We became engaged in a conversation saying, "What's it all about." "I am just passing through." "Yeah!" Then he asked, "What about you, have all of your desires been fulfilled in *LIFE*?" "Hell no, who has," I replied! "But, besides there being a few regrets, it's been a good and interesting ride." At this point, he just opened up verbally. This man appeared to be about 45 years old and had been homeless for 10 years. It was a gradual thing, stemming from drugs and alcohol. He knew all the angles for a free ride in life. Sooner or later, he became dependent and needed the system relative to his survival.

"Life's tough," he said. "Over the years, I've burnt all the bridges behind me including my family." "Mister, far worst then you have bounced back!" Sympathizing with him then saying, "But my brother, you're a white man." He was tall and lean, observed no physical limitations and lives in a society where Whites are the majority and rule.

He said, "I'd fare much better as a black man in my present status, especially around here." "Aw, I don't know about that but, why so?" "I'm just frowned upon being White and begging where it seems much more acceptable coming from a poor black person. That's just one more concern relative to their predicament!" "I guess so, when you've been beat down to the ground in all arenas by the oppressor since our existence in AMERICA. But, yes, I can see your point."

"Hey, it has been a good conversation but it's time to move on." Glancing over at the cab and noticing a lady standing close with a suitcase. I hollered from the distance, "Do you need a cab?" "Yes, I have a train to catch and need to get to Penn Station ASAP." "Well, my Man, here's a few bucks for you since saving on my lunch expense. Take care of yourself."

Story #57
Cab #1914 was dispatched to meet a MTA bus operator at North Avenue and Harford Road. All passengers had gotten off the bus upon my arrival; some were peeking through the windows, which aroused my curiosity. The bus driver was approached and asked, "What's going on?" "That elderly lady became nervous and extremely upset after missing her transfer stop and demanded a cab."

The bus driver asked, "Will you take her home?" "Only if she's no trouble," referring to wanting no confusion, "and can pay the cab fare." Unfortunately, these questions need asking after having been stuck with such passengers before.

Anyway, the lady was seated peacefully midway on the bus. She appeared to be in her eighties, about 5 feet 2 inches and possibly weighting 100 pounds. Her appearance was neat, wearing a long black coat, purse and had two well-used shopping bags, one inside the other with groceries. She was helped out of the seat, caught her balance and said, "Thank you Jesus," when off the bus. "Please be careful with my bags, Driver." They had a weathered look and appeared to be about 10 years old. At that point, the bus driver gave me the lady's home address. The driver said, "Thank you," as her passengers were re-boarding the bus. The elderly lady attempted to give directions and was told the bus driver had given me her home address. She said abruptly, "Excuse me, but I'm talking." "Yes Ma'am," being sorry to interrupt.

Her vision was poor as she tried focusing on landmarks en route to the house, never realizing where she was until on her street and block in East Baltimore. Then mumbling that those people were giving her no respect at all on that bus.

"How much driver?" My reply was $6.40. Honestly, never knew if this lady had money or not. She fumbled around in her purse for a good while, then searched her pockets finding four one-dollar bills. "How much did you say it was?" The fare was repeated as she continued her search for more money finding a folded five-dollar bill. "You were extremely nice and patient with me. Thank you sir, the change is your tip." She was assisted to her front door with pleasure. Old age can be a bitch!

Story #58

Some days it can be quite difficult figuring out where and what to eat. Basically, a half hour is taken every day, most times eating within certain establishments and when pressed in the cab. My choice on this particular day was Panda Express located on the Reisterstown Road Plaza parking lot; and I decided to eat in the cab after booking in that cab zone. The rule of thumb in this business is availability.

There was a call accepted from the computer just as I finished lunch. It was to meet an individual standing outside a disabled tractor-trailer truck at the intersection of Northern Parkway and Wabash. His destination was the truck terminal located in Jessup, Maryland.

He flagged as the cab approached. "That was fast," he said, and then repeated his destination that was already known from the computer. "Sir, the name of the game in this business is to respond quickly when calls are dispatched. If not, people will leave or find other means." This is a good job, around fifty bucks, so it is to my advantage to respond quickly.

"So, what happened to your truck?" "The gear box locked up. My dispatcher was contacted. He dispatched a tow truck and told me to catch a cab back to base. These trucks are pushed hard up and down the eastern seaboard. The owners are greedy and quite frankly become merciless with the drivers for not dropping their freight on time. Basically, these truck problems can be prevented if maintained properly."

"There's lot of money to be made in this industry...Trucks move the country! My company handles short and long runs up and down coast. The longer runs pay good, but many times it's difficult to get those jobs." "Why so?" "Man, I'm new to the company and the longer trips come with baggage." "What baggage?" "Well, you have to be in the loop, in addition to the in-kind-favors." "I hear you, Sir, say no more." "These days, corruption seems to be the way of the world. Anyway, I've done well since being in this industry. There's always work with my truck driving experiences somewhere." "That's an interesting perspective."

Story #59

Cab 1914 was dispatched to the shopping center in the 700 block Washington Boulevard. There, I was met by a middle-aged white couple who wanted to go to a street up in Morrell Park located west of I-95 off Washington Boulevard. It was a bitter cold day and they were glad to be in a cab. The lady said, "I'd rather deal with this coldness then snow any day." "I heard that, Miss!"

The lady was a bartender who worked around the Boulevard and Desota Road. She talked of her homeless friend who was an alcoholic. He refused shelter during this cold spell because he couldn't drink at will. The man died days later and was found frozen stiff with a newspaper over his face under I-95. "There's a colony of alcoholics and drug addicts who live under there year around. They come up periodically for whatever."

The detectives stopped in the bar telling her that according to the coroner he died from two heart attacks and there was no foul play involved. He probably would have survived but his body was filled with enormous amounts of infection. Oh well, that's the life he chose!

Story #60

This white guy about 30 years old approached the cab while sitting on the taxi stand at Broadway and Thames. "Where to Sir?" "Take me to the 2100 block of Lafayette Avenue." "Sir, east or west Lafayette Avenue." "I really don't know; my car was towed from the parking lot opposite Frederick Douglass Museum." "Oh, that towing place is in West Baltimore."

"What happened?" "I'm a bartender down here. There's normally an attendant on the lot where I park. Well, today he wasn't there. So, I parked anyway and got towed. The cost is unreal, would you believe $280.00." "Hey, that's a tough lesson to learn." "Yes it is, without a doubt!"

We traveled west on Franklin Street through downtown to the portion of US Route 40 West locally known as the *highway-to-nowhere*. Made a right turn onto Wheeler Avenue and another right at Lafayette.

"I can't remember the last time that I've been on this side of town. The plan was to leave my car in the neighborhood after paying my tow bill and have my friend pick me up. But, I'm not too sure now." "Man, your car will be okay; just don't leave anything of value in plain view. Really, that should be the case wherever you park."

"Hopefully you observed that this is a peaceful working class neighborhood where homeowners reside. Many have worked extremely hard for their accomplishments. Why are you so judgmental, because it's a neighborhood of Blacks? There are many folks whose education and accomplishments far exceed us both. Some have done extremely well. Has the mass media and Hollywood productions poisoned your mind to this degree?" "Sir, I'm sorry!"

Story #61
My normal Sunday morning routine is to walk and browse at the Farmers' Market underneath Interstate #83 between 10:30AM and 11:30AM. Basically, this is when the crowd

usually peaks. Occasionally I have a delicious cheese and artichoke omelet with coffee at Humpty Dumpty's that is located next to the roast beef and sausage stand. Then I get into shopping for fruits and vegetables and sometimes when the taste is there, a treat to live crabs. This fresh food market exemplifies the many different cultures of our City.

The cab was parked up on Fallsway under the Orleans Street Viaduct. As I approached, some people with groceries were noticed around the vehicle. "Sir, are you working?" one asked. "Yes, where would you like to go?" "There're two destinations. My girlfriend and I are going to the 7-11 on MLK Boulevard at Cathedral and he's going to Whole Foods in the vicinity of Falls Road and Kelley Avenue."

We tried communicating while en route. They were foreigners and taught in the Baltimore City Public School System as elementary school teachers. Saying to myself, really it was so difficult for me to understand them. They were asked to repeat themselves several times. You had to listen intently.

There is an awful lot of growth and development in children the first ten years of their lives. How in the world could they be teaching our children if they are not speaking the English language with its clearest pronunciation and understanding? To me, this is such an injustice.

What is the reason behind the massive hiring of so many foreign teachers for our city children? Is it *money* or has basic education become so unattractive on college campuses that we must advertise to the world that America needs teachers?

Story#62
Cab 1914 was flagged by a middle-aged black man in front of the main branch of the Enoch Pratt Free Library on Cathedral

Street. His destination was Northeast Market in East Baltimore.

While driving across the Orleans Street Viaduct, he said "From a distance Johns Hopkins Hospital looks like a city in itself rising through the ground with those tall, majestic buildings reaching to the heavens." "Hey, they think it is!" He went on to say, "It's a massive complex consisting of about 40 buildings and most are connected by either overhead walkways or underground tunnels. They have a massive security force with police and video cameras strategically stationed throughout the hospital campus."

He lives just north of the hospital off Broadway and has been active in his neighborhood organization for years. "The hospital has planned 50 years in the future, having purchased blocks of real estate over time. This move has contributed to the discomfort of many East Baltimoreans. Relocating has been rough for many having to uproot throughout the City and surrounding counties. For some, their adjustments were hard living away from family, friends and old neighborhoods."

"They definitely carry a lot of weight in the City! It's to my understanding that there's gonna be an East Baltimore Amtrak Station at the railroad's overpass on Broadway or in close proximity. Did you know that public housing and a branch library once occupied the land where the Orleans Street parking lot is located?" "Yes, I remember." "Well, it was swapped with Church Hospital's property that was located diagonally across the street. "Now, that's what you call power and influence! I guess that it's all for the good."

"Hopkins is known as the greatest hospital in the world relative to its research in medicine. Sir, as a cab driver I can attest that patients come from the world over. They are from many different cultures and have taken cabs from the hospital to the airport or Penn Station. Most patients say that their hospital experience is absolutely extraordinary, in other words priceless!"

"Hopkins contributes heavily to the business sector. There're lots of outside vendors that are needed and consequently depend on the facility to function. Many family members and friends stay in area hotels while patients are recuperating."

"Well, the hospital has come a long ways since I first started in the cab business. My cab driving days date back to when the Rotunda on Broadway was the hospital's main entrance. Howard Johnson Motor Inn was located where the Wilmer Eye Clinic is. Also, resident doctors with families lived within a fenced compound where the outpatient clinic is now located. There was no construction for years. Then all of a sudden, there would be five construction sites going on simultaneously. Like, they had no time to waste!" Soon, 1800 Orleans Street will be the hospital and emergency room's main entrance.

"Well, Hopkins has six campuses around the City which include the University. It's the number one employer in the Baltimore and Maryland private sector and definitely contributes to the functioning of this City." "Sir, I must agree!"

Story #63
It was so cold and the wind was just a howling on this particular winter day in January. Looking at people through the cab window shivering on the bus stops gave me chills to my spine. This poor stiff who appeared to be half frozen was standing on the number #3 bus stop at Loch Raven and Belvedere flagged. His destination was Garrison Boulevard and Barrington Road in the Forest Park section of the City.

He talked about how he made good money when employed as a cab driver in between complaining about the coldness. Then he changed the subject and discussed his sister who was recently divorced and was having her home remodeled. This work was performed by him and his brother, they were settling today. We were going to the Barrington Road address for the money.

The brother owned the home improvement business; naturally he got most of the money for the project. His share was $9,000 and he was going to get the cash, now! Once at the Barrington Road address the meter read $23.00. He gave me $17.00 and told me to hold tight for the rest and that he might possibly be going somewhere else. "No problem, I'll be here."

The cab was positioned directly in front of the house for observation purposes. He finally came out of this framed porch house with a well-guarded brown paper bag tightly secured in his right hand. His next destination was Walgreens drugstore at Liberty Heights and Garrison. I had to peek to the backseat while driving, it being absolutely noisy. And quite frankly, curiosity got the best of me noticing him counting one-hundred bills pleasurably! Saying, "Wild, I know I'm gonna get a good tip, huh." "Here's a fifty, thanks." "And thanks to you too, Sir."

Story #64
The dispatcher was calling for cabs at the zoo. There, the cab was approached by a middle-aged black woman with three children. Her destination was Mello Court down in the inner city near Hopkins Hospital. She sat up front while the children were fighting over who's gonna have the window seats in the back.

"They were promised this trip to the zoo after completing my nine months treatment program at Genesis IV. Man was that tough, one is truly regimented there. The building is 100 percent maintained by its clients, even the preparation of meals. The good thing about this program was that my children were with me.

"This place was located in Maryland out in the middle of nowhere, like on a farm. There was no contact with the outside world unless you had a doctor's appointment. You only had visitors every other Sunday after a 30-day blackout.

"What was truly unfair about the program was everybody being put on lockdown because someone broke the rules, like having a hidden cell phone. But I had to grit my teeth because I was getting help and my children were housed and fed. This program also enabled me to save a good portion of my welfare check while getting this monkey off my back! It was hard, damn hard, but I'm clean now and gonna stay that way. I'm just too damn old to go through that shit again."

"Miss, I believe you after opening up and telling me all that." Then she said, "One of the greatest things throughout the entire ordeal was the support of my children and a friend on the outside who wrote and visited on a regular basis. Those factors, along with prayer and my counselor contributed to me successfully completing the program.

"There was more than once that I was ready to pack my shit and get out of there!" "I hear you Miss." "Mister, I wasn't court ordered. I just became sick and tired of the lifestyle! I really started realizing how dear my children are to me and that my character will contribute to the successes or failures in their lives. I'm thankful to the program. I'm still on the welfare but I have a job and through the section-8 program

I'm able to rent a house up in Waverly." "That's great!" I sincerely hope she makes it.

Story #65

My cab was precariously parked at the southwest corner of Washington and McElderry Streets waiting to get on Hopkins' illegal cabstand in the next block because of construction on the property. This is a real cat and mouse game for the drivers. Cabs stage there until the transportation starter whistles for their services at the main entrance of the hospital or they are chased by the parking ticket lady from Baltimore City's Traffic Division.

This slim white guy about 25 years old rushed hurriedly toward the cab telling me he needed my services and that he's running late. The guy didn't know the exact address, so instructions were given when and where to turn. He appeared to be a reformed drug addict.

He said, "Step on it Pop." at the intersection on Chester and Fayette Streets. That *Pop shit* didn't settle very well with me but nothing was said regarding that issue. "Sir, the light's red, gas will be applied once the light changes."

His final destination was St. Elizabeth of Hungary Catholic Church located at Lakewood and Baltimore Streets. Some hospitals and churches in the metropolitan area run federally funded drug and alcohol rehab programs.

He paid the fare, and then joined others assembled on the Lakewood Street side of the church. They were periodically sipping out of their soda bottles and smoking cigarettes. Meanwhile, classes of elementary students led by their teachers in double lines and neatly dressed in their school uniforms were returning from recess in Patterson Park. The children made notice of this motley group of individuals outside the church as they passed. The proximity was just too close to the school's environment.

Story #66

This middle-aged man who first looked at his watch, then at me and back to his watch signaled at the intersection of Greenmount Avenue and Madison Street. His destination was the 200 block E. Lexington Street. He had been arrested for driving while intoxicated and had just been released from jail. Presently, he was going to see a lawyer who had been recommended.

He spoke with a broken accent, later revealing that he was Brazilian and asked to use my cell phone. The call was to his company asking for the day off. After hanging up, he told me that his mouth got him locked up. The cop wasn't going to arrest him until being cursed out, which drew a crowd. He kept saying, "Why didn't I just shut up!"

Anyway, he was told of me once being a Baltimore City Policeman and that driving is definitely a privilege. "Sir, it doesn't take much for the state to revoke your driver's license." The legal costs can be unbelievable and there's still a hearing with the Department of Motor Vehicles, even if found not guilty by the courts. Motor Vehicles has a completely different set of guidelines than the courts. "Sir, driving while intoxicated is a very serious charge and can haunt one for the rest of their life depending upon the circumstances."

"Driver, I'm a poor man and my job is on the line." "Good luck to you Sir, I'd advise you to find money from somewhere and get yourself a very good lawyer who specializes in DWI cases."

Story #67
The Preakness Stakes is Baltimore and Maryland's largest single day event. This horse race is the second leg of the US Triple Crown. It's been held at the Pimlico Racetrack on the third Saturday in May for over 100 years. Lately the annual crowds have been estimated to be approximately well over 120,000 people.

The track does extremely well Preakness week, drawing horse lovers, racetrack followers and its Triple Crown fans. In addition, it draws an enormous amount of partygoers, as does the tourist traps that surround the Inner Harbor. Our State flower, the Black-Eye Susan is also a famous Maryland drink at many restaurants and bars that week. There are all kinds of activities in town Preakness Week including the Flower Mart, the Preakness Parade and the crab race that is held at Lexington Market.

Those that desire prime locations at the racetrack's infield start heading for Pimlico as early as 3AM. Coolers filled with beer could be taken to the infield up until being banned there recently. That move was inevitable...they partied hard with alcohol, drugs and whatever. Fistfights broke out, ladies flashed their boobs and people were pissing everywhere. You name it, it was happening. Many a person (men and women) had to be cartwheeled from the infield. Some never even saw one actual horserace period. *The infield crowd was becoming outrageously WILD!*

The cab was flagged around O'Donnell Square by two young ladies and a guy in front of Nacho Mama's Restaurant. They were rather tipsy! One chick was hugged up and appeared rather sweet on the dude. They sat in the back while the other lady sat up front with me. "Power Plant Live, please?"

The lady up front was friendly and projected a vivid personality. She said, "The town is rocking and rolling tonight, people are everywhere." "Yeah, tell me about it, it's the Friday night before the Preakness stakes."

"My girlfriend and I decided to barhop and enjoy the excitement generated from this crowd of visitors to the City. Really, we've been partying hard and want to have some fun. Actually, we want to do that dude in the back but he's acting like a *PUSSY* and doesn't seem to be cooperating." *I said, "What are you kidding me; you want to do what?"* I turned and faced her, damn near having an accident! "Yeah, he's kinda drunk but I believe he's scared and can't fuck." "*Oh!*"

At this point, I was going along with the flow. This situation is becoming quite interesting. "That's why, we can't get the response we'd like," she said, "Maybe it'll happen," then smiled showing these perfectly beautiful pearly white teeth and saying "Maybe it won't!" "Your teeth are absolutely gorgeous." "Thanks, my girlfriend and I are dental students." "Here in Baltimore?" "Yep!" I just laughed...

Anyway, after paying the fare and while leaving the cab, her black thongs were riding high above the waistline of her jeans. *Unbelievable, this is definitely the dream of most men, REALLY!* Hey, they were nice looking and ready, rather juiced up and wanted some action from this particular guy and he's laid back there hemming and hawing drunk. *All I can say as a dreamer and fantasying is my, my, my!*

Story #68
New Year's Eve is always GOOD! Cab services become hot and heavy around 9:30PM and last throughout the night. People are everywhere! They line the shores of the Inner Harbor from Canton to Federal Hill and beyond. All elevated

vantage points in the vicinity of downtown are utilized; people's focuses are on the Inner Harbor fireworks. Many restaurants are packed as well as hotels, clubs and partying in private homes. It's a big money-maker for cab drivers because most people are partying hard and refuse to stay put at any one location.

The annual New Years' Eve fireworks started a few years before my first book entitled *Hey Cabbie,* was self-published in 1984. Baltimore's downtown, then, was a ghost town after 6PM. The City Fathers wanted nightlife downtown to attract masses of people to various public and private venues. The first attractions were the Baltimore City Fair, the Hyatt Hotel, the Convention Center, the National Aquarium and the World Trade Center. Their vision and efforts have been well received to this date!

During that time period, downtown Baltimore shifted from the Howard/Lexington Street corridor to Lombard/Pratt Streets south and President Street to Martin Luther King Boulevard east to west respectively, including the Inner Harbor.

The major holidays drew masses of people to the harbor. Many people spent their entire day relaxing, shopping and strolling the harbor's promenade. The restaurant business boomed. People waited in lines outside of establishments for tables. The Inner Harbor's business was no joke to its employees. Tourists and conventioneers were attracted and they loved our City!

Also, there was a state of the arts movie house at the intersection of Market and Lombard. Here, one could park within the complex, catch the parking lot's elevator and in seconds be within the theatre's lobby.

That was then and this is now! The recession, high unemployment and crime have plagued our City. The movie theatre is long gone. Many businesses have relocated to what is considered the City's newest jewel, Harbor East. We have lost a good percentage of our population to the surrounding counties and the local news media don't paint a pretty picture when it comes to crime, especially when it concerns the Harbor.

There's a big divide between the *'haves'* and *'have nots'*. The police are put on high alert when it's known that the *have nots* are coming to the Inner Harbor. Baltimore City's black population is well over 65 percent.

New Year's Eve fireworks draw a heavy cross-cultural mix of citizenry from across the Baltimore Metropolitan Area. This event brings out a huge show of force, which includes unformed police, mounted and motorcycled patrol and their equipment. Streets are barricaded, large floodlights are strategically placed and a mobile jail is positioned in close proximity. They are prepared and ready for the action! The only thing that appears to be missing is riot helmets and long crowd control batons.

This well dressed middle-aged white couple, tuxedo and all, flagged at the intersection of Lombard and Light Streets. They were sharp, somewhat tipsy and full of joy for the evening. Their destination was Canton Square. He said, "Man, it's been absolutely hell in trying to get a cab!

"We intentionally left our car home and wanted to cab it for the evening. It was no problem in getting to our affair at the Hyatt. But, after leaving the hotel, no cabs were to be found, police had cordoned off the surrounding streets. The only street in the immediate vicinity that was open was Light Street South and there all cabs zoomed by hired!

"So, we walked and were harassed by the police at pedestrian detours. They actually told us in abrupt tones where we could and could not cross the street. Finally, we were able to get on Calvert at Pratt, this street was also closed to vehicle traffic and these huge spotlights beamed down on us from Redwood at Calvert, everything was lit up and police were everywhere." The lady said, "This is definitely a turn off. I know that the police are here to protect and serve but I actually feel like I'm under military detention in a war zone. This is scary. I sincerely hope they come up with a better plan for policing the Inner Harbor's major events in the future." Actually, I was real nervous, also.

Story #69

The day after Baltimore's two historic blizzard snowstorms was rough. The main arteries throughout the City were barely becoming passable. Some had just a single path while others had lanes for inbound and outbound traffic. The City had become immobile from these two snowstorms totaling well over forty inches. Residents were told by our new Mayor Stephanie Rawlings-Blake, who had only been in office for a week, to "band together, work collectively and we will get through this."

Our City was declared a disaster by the Federal Government's standards. Earth moving equipment and bobcats were brought in to begin the mammoth task of clearing streets in order to make the City functional again. Man-made mountains of snow were erected at most intersections and on vacant lots. The small streets looked like tributaries feeding into the City's main arteries.

The Mayor enacted phase three of the snow emergency plan, which meant only emergency vehicles were permitted on the streets of Baltimore and violators would be arrested. The clearing of cars from snow emergency routes caused massive problems; people could not locate their vehicles for days.

While stopped for the eastbound traffic light at University Parkway and North Charles, this middle- aged black man ran toward the cab needing my services. His car had been towed off a snow emergency route and he was told by the police that it was on a parking lot in the 900 block East 39th Street. "There's no 900 block East 39th, Mister, but the same roadway becomes Argonne Drive once it crosses Old York Road. There's a large school parking lot located at 900 Argonne Drive." "Take me there, let's search the lot together." His car was not to be found. "Take me to my mother's at 22nd and Kirk; there I'll use the phone to call the City for the exact location of my car. I may need a lift to Randallstown, then on to work in Linthicum."

He was given my card for future service and was picked up less than a half hour later after being told that the car was on Lot A next to the Fallsway's impound lot. Not knowing the exact location of Lot A, a female police officer at the impound lot told us it was where Farmer's Market is held on Sunday's.

You should have seen the joy on this man's face when we found his car and it was well understood. No ticket was affixed but that's not saying one won't be issued. He gave me $50.00 for sticking with him, not bad for less than an hour's work. Although, the cab rides to Randallstown and then on to his U.S Postal job in Linthicum would have paid much more; helping the man while in crisis was just really rewarding to me.

Story #70
My passenger's destination was Eddies Supermarket in Roland Park. Cross Keys' taxi zone was booked into while

traveling up Roland Avenue. The fare was paid and a taxi access call was accepted in The Village of Cross Keys, which was a little unusual. Rarely are taxi access calls dispatched from that location because of its high socio-economic status.

I stopped at the gatehouse to obtain the exact location of the street dispatched. A white lady about 75 years old assisted by a walker that had tennis balls on the front legs was standing by a row of garages opposite condo units when I arrived. She was beautifully dressed wearing a blue pants suit. Her outfit was offset with a lovely brooch and gold jewelry.

While I was exiting the cab to assist her, a wet horseshoe stain was noticed around the lady's crotch. Once seated, she let me know with her southern drawl that her home was North Carolina. "Prior to your arrival, the company called saying the cab is five minutes away. That was 45 minutes ago. Driver, I'm late for my appointment at Mercy Hospital. Hopefully, my doctor will still see me."

She had returned to her condo and recalled the cab company after 20 minutes had elapsed. The wait and walk outside while anticipating the cab's arrival contributed to her urinating on herself because of health issues. An apology was extended to this lady!

Story #71
Stopped directly behind this old station wagon at the intersection of Erdman Avenue and Sinclair Lane. The rear window was down with the backseat facing me. These white people appeared to be extremely poor and disadvantaged. Occupying the rear seat was a boy about 6 years old and in desperate need of a haircut.

He had a nice friendly smile waving his hand from left to right saying, "Hi nigger." The child was totally ignored, saying to myself that the "N" word was removed from the English language. Which is total bullshit! Many Blacks are still referred to as 'niggers' all over the world up to this present day. Anyway, this has to be learned behavior, undoubtedly. Really, what do his parents discuss about the black race in his presence. Thinking what will his views be of the black race as he matures through life.

This incident led me to thinking how prevalent racism and discrimination is in our City. Racism tops the chart, followed by money. Just look at the disparity in the abundant luxury gated high-rise condos and apartment buildings in downtown Baltimore, prestigious places of entertainment and socialization, isolated City neighborhoods setup like mazes designed by purpose for *them*, as compared to low-paying jobs that minorities hold, severe public school problems, police encounters and unreal housing situations. This is definitely a divide!

Anyway, the child waved again saying, "Hi, nigger, nigger, nigger." I just regrouped and waved back. He knows no better thinking to myself. It's a shame - it is what it is and always will be. It amazes me how President Obama ever got elected!

Story#72

It was slow - *actually business stunk*. I had been sitting on 7/11's parking lot located at Broadway and Lombard for a while. Boredom started to set in, the mind wonders, thinking how well this day could have been spent anywhere besides sitting around in this cab empty. But, it's paramount that you stay focused! The greater portion of my income can be made during any segment of the shift. You never know when.

The decision was made to get a corn beef on rye from Attman's Delicatessen in Jew Town on Lombard Street. Dammit, it never fails; just as I was parking a man wearing a yarmulke approached and asked was I working. "Where are you going, Sir?" "Pikesville, I'm in a hurry!" Hey, this is what it's all about - later for lunch. Pikesville is a thirty-plus dollars job.

The radio was tuned to 95.9 FM when the man entered. A local DJ played the piece with President Obama singing Al Green's rendition of *Let's Stay Together*. He said, "Obama is absolutely brilliant, what better way could he have opened his 2012 presidential campaign." "Hey, he has to be a helluva chess player. I wonder what his next move is."

"The man has done an admirable job considering what was handed over from the Bush Administration. His accomplishments are numerous including the health care bill, career training for laid-off workers and expanding the Pell grant loans. In addition to ending the war in Iraq, increasing bank depositors' insurance; and the finding and doing away with America's number one criminal, Bin Laden." "You know, he would really capture the American voters if gas prices would stop escalating. Maybe that's the last dance before the big November show!"

"His lack of respect from white America is plain and simple, *he's a black man holding the white man's most powerful seat in this country and quite frankly the world* and *they can't stand it!* Right now, the Republicans are battling hard and dirty to come up with a viable presidential candidate. I can't wait for the presidential debates between President Obama and their candidate. It seems like the best debates would be between the President and Newt Gingrich but that doesn't seem likely at this point."

"I'm extremely proud of the President as are millions of people - black and white- regardless of the outcome concerning this November's Presidential Election. One term or not, he out smarted *them* entirely winning the highest seat of the land in 2008. You don't get any heavier than that! But, the way things are proceeding with the Republicans he's gonna be around to 2016."

"Anyway, exactly where to in Pikesville, Sir?" "Walgreens drugstore located at Reisterstown and Old Court Road." "Hey, may the best man win in November for the sake of our country!"

Story #73

The fare's destination was the foot of Broadway in Fells Point. It was the Friday night before the 4th of July; crowds were lined up outside the bars in the sweltering heat. The traffic light changed several times with no movement. Basically, we had to inch down Broadway with traffic being horrendous on this single lane street.

Due to the backup, my passengers decided to pay and get out of the cab in traffic about two car lengths before Aliceanna Street by the Subway restaurant. This hillbilly in a pickup truck directly behind the cab started honking his horn like some crazy-ass madman. He then hollered out the window, "Pull the goddamn cab over." "My reply was over where?"
He then deliberately hit the cab in the rear with his vehicle. I jumped out of the cab angry and having the male passenger as backup. Shouting, "What the fuck wrong with you man!" Instantly, my cell phone camera focused on him and his license tag, both were recorded. The police were then called with the phone on speaker.

He appeared high but realized the crowd forming was in my favor and the police had been summoned. So, he jumped back in his truck and left the scene. My cab bumper showed no damage after assessing the situation. It was the Friday night over a holiday weekend. The cops hadn't shown up after 30 minutes. My decision was to leave and go back to work. The money's out here and needed!

Believe me, it can be absolutely mind-boggling when the bars and nightclubs in Fells Point are at full throttle! There's a lot of action down here. Many infractions of the law are either overlooked or downsized.

Story #74

My eye caught the attention of a lovely light-skinned African American lady about 5'8" and around 40 years old. This chick was wearing a white linen skirt and blouse and had shoulder length blown hair. Her outfit was accented with a stylish handbag, matching shoes and sporting fashionable sunglasses. She was standing curbside in front of The Gallery and flagged when the traffic light changed at the intersection of Pratt and Calvert Streets.

"My you look nice." "Thank you Sir. Take me to Penn Station, please." While en route, we became engaged in conversation. She was from the Bahamas and had met someone who was on vacation there. They talked and eventually he wired her travel expenses to Baltimore. This was her first time to the Mid-Atlantic Region. She was going home soon and wanted to see Washington D.C.

She asked, "Are you familiar with Washington?" "Yes, I once had a tour guide business for Baltimore City Schools. Occasionally, my services were called upon for trips to D.C.

They study the Federal government in the fifth grade."
"Really," she said, "that's great. I guess that you know the
district rather well." "I'm okay," with a smile.

"So, where's the friend?" "Oh, he's working." "That's
unfortunate; you're bound to attract someone's attention as
lovely as you look venturing around D.C. all alone." "Well, I
certainly wanted him to come along but he just couldn't."
"Will you be comfortable?" "Yes I'm okay," she said with
confidence.

At this point, we were traveling north on Calvert crossing Mt.
Royal and thinking to myself - just go for it! We introduced
ourselves. Her name was Adronna. I asked her, "What's your
take if I accompanied you to D.C. as your guide pointing out
the main attractions." We had been having a great
conversation. Then, she said, "Sure, why not and thank you at
least I won't be alone." *Hey, it's becoming interesting!*

The cab was parked in the 1700 block of St. Paul. We caught
the Marc train to D.C. All day Metro passes were purchased
at Union Station. Also, it was suggested that she purchase a
disposable camera for keepsake memories. We took the train
to Federal Triangle. Pictures were taken of her on the mall
with the Washington Monument and Lincoln Memorial as
backdrops.

We ventured on to the Smithsonian's Museum of American
History. Later walked to the Post Office Pavilion on
Pennsylvania Avenue, caught the elevator to the top of the
tower and got a bird's eye view of the Federal City. It was a
sunny crystal clear sky blue day and the City could be seen in
all directions to its horizon. She said, "It's amazing seeing how
the street patterns lead into the traffic circles and squares
around buildings and monuments." We left there and walked
to The White House.

This had been one enjoyable day but it was becoming tiring. So, we caught a cab to H Street in Chinatown for dinner. We had cocktails and talked for a good while before ordering dinner. The decision was made to meet the next day at Tapas Teatro Restaurant on Charles Street for lunch. . We smiled at one another, pleasurably, after making that decision. She excused herself after eating and said, "I'm going to the lady's room to regroup and to make a phone call."

We left the restaurant and rode the Metro back to Union Station. She browsed the ladies apparel shops while I sat in the station's waiting area for the next train to Baltimore. It was a good relaxing ride back to the City. She got quite comfortable and started talking softly. Then rested her head on my shoulder after giving me an affectionate kiss and looking me in the eyes saying "Thank you for a wonderful day!"

Story #75
Usually, Sunday morning business consists of early runs to the airport or church work. The dispatcher posted on my screen that cabs were needed in the vicinity of Clifton Park. Cab 1914 picked up this lady dressed in black standing on the bus stop at the intersection of Harford and The Alameda. "Where to Miss?" "Huber Memorial Baptist Church located York Road at Bellona."

This middle-aged lady, who was well dressed with bible in tote, hummed to the radio's church music after she became comfortable. She said, "I'm running late, service started at 7:30 AM." "Miss, I'll do my best. Like, what time do you get up?" "Well, I like to relax on Sundays. So, I get up around 5:30 AM to attend early church. This enables me to enjoy the rest of my day."

"Do you attend Church?" "Not really, but I'm a Christian and do believe." "Our preacher's name is P.M. Smith. Have you ever heard of him?" "Yes, we worked together many years ago in the old Post Office on Calvert Street. I must say, he's really made a name for himself and has done extremely well relative to his calling. Occasionally, he's caught early Sunday mornings on television. To me, his growth is unbelievable!"

"Mister, he can really preach the word. His interpretation of scripture into today's realistic world is quite timely. It is quite obvious that he made the right decision when giving up law. You know, he's in tune with his congregation and their needs as they are with his. He recognizes achievers and announces their accomplishments to the church.

"He often talks of his childhood roots. Actually, he wants you to know about him and his family. Matter of fact, he still resides within the core of East Baltimore. The congregation is made up of a cross section of Blacks. They come from all over but the majority is from East Baltimore.

"The Reverend emphasizes the importance of family and education. He repeatedly says *it's the structure of it all. Our children are the fruit. They need the father and mother steering the helm together in the right direction of all aspects in their lives.*

"We've definitely outgrown our present location. Seats are rarely available at either service. The plan is to build a new sanctuary on the land acquired at Belvedere and Loch Raven along with a school and other necessary building." "Well, the Reverend P.M. Smith certainly appears inspirational." "Sir, please come and visit us!" "Yes Ma'am, I will... "

Story #76
My computer screen indicated that Mercy Hospital needed cabs at the main entrance. The hospital's transportation person approached after I pulled onto the driveway and asked would a voucher be acceptable for payment. "Sure!" "There's a lady being discharged from labor and delivery. I'll be right back." She returned with what appeared to be a family - the new mother in a wheelchair, the baby secured in a car seat on her lap and the father by her side.

This situation generated déjà vu. Many years ago to this day my son was born. Those memories are oh, so vivid. I felt amazed, accomplished and satisfied as a father, especially since my first-born was a boy. You didn't know the child's sex back in those days until birth and witnessing the event was taboo.

I'd loved to have seen the birth of my children, especially my daughter who is special. Maybe, we would have been aware of any complications during delivery had I been present, that were not observed until some two years later when lack of motor skills was noticed.

Although I have been divorced for many years, my children have always been my life. Now, they are middle-aged adults and have turned out rather well. It wasn't at all easy, God knows! Good parental guidance and support contributed to their successes. My son is married and has a family and daughter lives with her mother. Both are independent and gainfully employed.

Monica is sweet, loveable and very thoughtful. She's on time about everything, extremely conscientious about her job and has become one excellent shopper. The shopping trait definitely comes from her mother.

Jonathan's preferred sport is basketball. He took me to see the Wizards and dinner in D.C. We had a great time together. Also, my son's family and Monica treated us to Father's Day Brunch at the Marriott Waterfront Hotel. **These events in conjunction with many other memorable occasions make you feel loved and appreciated. My children!**

Anyway "Miss, congratulations, where to?" "The 2800 block Gwynns Falls Parkway. That's west of Mondawmin Mall and Coppin State University's new gymnasium." "What did you have?" "It's a healthy boy, weighing seven pounds." "Wild, he's a big one, huh." It was a good ride uptown. They were having a soft and pleasant conversation. I had noticed them when adjusting the rearview mirror, both admiring their newborn and kissing.

At their destination, he searched through his pocket and gave me a couple dollars extra over and above the voucher's fee. He was thanked with pleasure and I peeped at their cute little boy. I said, "Take good care of your family, young Man" "...Thank you, Sir!"

Story #77
Cab 1914 was dispatched to the new Giant food market located on 41st Street. It's across the street from the Royal Farms Store. I was met by an elderly white lady with a couple of bags. "Hello driver, please take me to the Keswick Nursing Home located a couple of blocks down the road on 40th Street."

She said, "That store, without a doubt is a grocery shoppers' dream! I mean they have everything. Plus, its huge, it has to be twice the size of their Rotunda store. The specialty departments, gourmet meats, seafood and delicatessen are superb, like on the same plateau as Whole Foods and Eddies

Supermarket." "Really, that's saying something, I haven't shopped there yet. But, Miss, it's gonna take some time for me getting used to their new location. I really liked Giant when it was located in that Rotunda Mall."

"Well, let me get myself together. I'm going to visit my husband of fifty years. This is his third week there rehabbing. Keswick is a wonderful place. It's like Baltimore's Cadillac of nursing homes. I visit him daily. He is loved dearly but this routine is really wearing me out at this age. But, I feel that my presence is needed, it definitely shows concern."

"I hear you, Miss. Recently, my mother rehabbed there after a brief stay at Sinai Hospital. She had several complications. Our major concern was fluid buildup that contributed to heart concerns and low oxygen intake. The staff, medication and physical therapy did wonders along with a good family support system."

"She glowed when released after thirty days of constant care. The fluid was gone and she no longer needed to be on oxygen. Like, they added years to her life. Our main objective is to keep her confidence intact and exercise of some sort is a daily must! She lives with my brother's family. The house is full of life, there are constant household activities that she is involved in and she's happy."

"Driver, that's wonderful! Your success story about your mother has certainly uplifted me. There's also tremendous progress in my husband's situation. My family can't wait to for him come home." "How much driver?" "Miss, the ride's on me, God Bless you...All the best to your husband!" "Thank you, sir."

Story #78

Lately, this region has been experiencing some strange weather conditions. Hurricanes are not unusual but rare for the Mid-Atlantic States. They seem to have much more of an impact in the Caribbean and those states that border the Gulf of Mexico. Every now and then, one's course is charted traveling the United States' coastal line of the Atlantic Ocean.

Hurricane Irene with a diameter of 500 miles touched the Atlantic Ocean's shores of North Carolina with Washington D.C. and Baltimore in its direct path. It continued on in a northeasterly direction to Canada.

The City put its hurricane plan to work. Sand bags were distributed to the neighborhoods of East Harbor and Fells Point. Also, parking was prohibited in those areas south of Fleet Street. We received freight tankers of water from this severe storm. The heavy rain and high winds caused trees to uproot and basement flooding to numerous homes and commercial businesses. But, Fells Point and surrounding neighborhoods were spared the anticipated street flooding and severe damage from this hurricane.

Hundreds of thousands of homes in the metropolitan area were without electricity, some for weeks! This problem caused people to double up with family and friends whose electricity and lights were intact. Some even stayed in hotels until the problems were rectified.

In the days that followed, cleanup was extremely slow, primarily because of the numerous downed trees and electrical wires. The Governor and Mayor advised people to come out in cases of emergencies only. The biggest problem around here appeared to be lack of electrical power in entire neighborhoods, which contributed to total blackouts.

The cab business was extremely slow, people were out but they weren't riding. So, consequently you make the best of it. My plan throughout the course of the days was to sit on the cabstand at University Hospital after purchasing lunch at Lexington market.

This middle-aged white lady approached just as I finished lunch. Her request was Penn Station. I did not notice until later that a large blue plastic tote bag was in her possession. She had reservations on the Acela to Manhattan and wanted to change to something earlier. The travel agent informed her that nothing was available and that all trains to the north were cancelled because of track flooding. "Let's try the airlines then," and instructed me to head in that direction. There again, nothing was available because of the hurricane's devastation.

She was still in conversation with her travel agent, then asked with a laugh, "Would you be interested in a round trip to New York City?" Being well aware of transportation problems, but as an experienced cabbie never to intervene into people's conversations unless there's an opening or invited, the request was anticipated.

My reply without hesitation was yes, sure without a doubt, not even considering the mechanical aspect of the cab. The excitement was overwhelming, to actually be considered for such a trip. This is the first ever of such magnitude. Just imagine roundtrip cost from Baltimore to New York City in a taxicab. Hey, that's a good piece of change... **It's also the dream of any cabbie!**

This cab is a 2002 Ford Crown Victoria, subject to Maryland State and Public Service Commission inspections annually. The vehicle has passed all tests but its commercial use contributes to excessive wear and tear mechanically much more then family owned cars. It has been utilized as a cab for five years and is soon up for replacement. The life for a cab in Baltimore City is 10 years from the manufacturer's date. The decision was reaffirmed in my mind after weighing all aspects before starting the trip.

We introduced ourselves after coming to an agreement on the fare. It was unbelievable what we agreed on excluding tolls and even better that it was going to be squared off with cash! The necessary calls were made concerning her change of transportation plans. Then she appeared to be catching up on phone calls with family and friends.

Later, we talked. I was told that she's a courier of human body parts. Inside the blue quilted tote bag in her immediate possession is a small lunch type cooler with human bone marrow on ice. Being spellbound saying, "You're shittin' me, I mean. . . sorry, really?" She said, "This can be a life or death situation for the recipient, so it's extremely crucial that we arrive at the hospital on time." Her role was serious; telephone calls had to be made periodically.

She's a volunteer who travels abroad occasionally on such missions. All expenses are paid by various fund raising organizations. She treasures her contribution to such a worthy cause in society. Saying there's nothing materialistic, nor is there any amount of money that would express her appreciation.

Primarily, because of the general slowdown from the hurricane, it was a smooth ride with traffic at a minimum all the way to Manhattan. It's rare to cruise through Delaware without encountering severe traffic backups in both directions of the toll plaza. Actually, we were coming out the Lincoln Tunnel and on 42nd Street just shy of 3 hours. The hospital was in the vicinity of First Avenue and 68th Street. The City has a grid format that made it easy to find.

The transfer of the bone marrow and paperwork took approximately 15 minutes. While in the hospital, she inquired about restaurants in the vicinity. We cruised 1st Avenue between 68th and 75th Streets finding a nice little Italian restaurant. The cultural ambience was unreal.

We talked over cocktails before dinner. It was to my surprise to hear that she has lived in Ashburton for 20 years. This neighborhood was once known as the gold coast for African Americans; that was some 50 years ago. She is self-employed as a consultant, has a degree in cultural arts and is a board member to a local theatre. Also, she has a family with two children who attend private schools.

The drive home was quite comfortable. She requested to sit up front on the return trip. Then kicked her shoes off and sat Indian style on the seat. We talked or should it be said that she talked the most en route to Baltimore. Discussing the City's politics, the arts and touched upon some family matters. There was only one bottle of water left, which was shared.

Once in Baltimore, she asked me to stop pass Bank of America's ATM because additional money was needed. She was driven home, finalizing the cab fare and assisted to the door. My gratitude was sincerely expressed for the job!

Story #79
The City is preparing for its first Grand Prix Car Race, EVER! Baltimore will have the contract for the next five years. Media coverage and exposure to Baltimore City is absolutely priceless. Every aspect of the hospitality industry will flourish. Hotels in the City and surroundings counties including Annapolis and Washington D.C. will be booked, maybe overbooked, that's the plan. This three-day event is to attract well over 100,000 people.

Many Baltimoreans are not in tune with the enormous expense attached to the Grand Prix. Many say that money should be earmarked for other essential projects in this poor struggling City. Lately, City residents have been nickel and dimed for everything! As a cab driver though, anything that brings money to this City is WELCOMED!

Due to road construction on Pratt Street, I veered around it by driving through upper Federal Hill. The cab was flagged by two white yuppies when turning from Montgomery onto Light Street. "We're looking for a good strip bar; which would you recommend, the bars on The Block or Scores." This request was odd because they were of the opposite sex. "Lately, my customers have been directing me to Scores." "Take us there."

"We're lawyers, you know. He's from Philadelphia and I'm a criminal lawyer working for one of Baltimore's prestigious law firms." "Who, where?" "I'd rather not say."

"He's dying to be teased by a stripper, I don't know why." Then she said in whisper, "He desires for me go back to our law school days. Maybe," she then hesitated while thinking and said, "I don't know what his motive is. We graduated a few years ago, plus I'm married." "Oh yeah!"

"So, what will you do while he's being entertained?" "Actually, I really don't know besides having some highballs. I'm not going to let myself get too tipsy because I don't want my kinkiness exposed. Hey, I might get up and dance on the tabletop if the atmosphere's right and the music's tantalizing. Maybe, just sit and watch the stripper tease him with her provocative movements especially if he gets a lap dance. Like, I said, I really don't know. I'll just play it by ear."

Thinking to myself, if time had only permitted, this cab would have been parked, most definitely just to observe her role in this episode. It's been a rough day and I must stay focused on the GOAL. They gave me an excellent tip..."Have fun you two!"

Story #80

While cruising in the vicinity of Lexington Market, I became hungry and had a taste for a couple of chili hotdogs from Konstant's stall in the market. Ironically, the cab was parked illegally at the fire hydrant. But, for some reason, I just sat there in the cab and started *people-watching* at the corner of Eutaw and Lexington Streets in front of the peanut stand.

It's can be absolutely amazing watching the hustlers go about their trades from the Muslim brother selling newspapers and bean pies, street vendors, to the alcoholics, religious sidewalk preachers, people with their entire life in the bus shelter and the selling of loose cigarettes at two for a dollar, drugs and whatever. These types of activities can be found within certain neighborhoods throughout the City. I often wondered what is the fate of our people in the next two decades in conjunction with many other serious circumstances.

Suddenly, a faint tap on the front passenger's side window was heard. I turned and noticed this sweet looking brown-skinned petite lady needing my services. "Sir, are you working?" "Yes, get in," saying to myself so much for those hotdogs. Her destination was near Morgan State University. We became involved in a pleasant conversation immediately. This woman had personality!

We became so relaxed while talking that she positioned herself in the middle of the backseat and moved closer to the partition. The rearview mirror was refocused while driving north on Calvert Street. She could be felt eyeing the contents on the front seat and my PSC badge. She said, "I remember you, I purchased an autographed copy of *Hey Cabbie* from you years ago from Greetings and Readings. It was an interesting read, rather raw and dirty, but I really couldn't put the book down. I never knew what the next episode would bring. Thaddeus, how did the book do?"

"Well, I'm rather proud of *Hey Cabbie* and its accomplishments. The book did extremely well in the Baltimore Metropolitan Area and beyond. It was #1 in demand at the Enoch Pratt Free Library for 10 straight weeks beginning June 2, 1985; beating out Lee Iacocca's book *An Autobiography,* President and CEO of Chrysler Corporation." "Wild, that's pretty impressive," she said! "Yeah, I had my 15 minutes of fame."

"My biggest challenge was getting the book off the shelf and into the hands of the consumer. The plan was to create a demand for the book prior to its distribution. Anita Lewis, News American's reporter, read the manuscript and interviewed me over lunch at Harbor Place. She later wrote a full-page spread on the local fold of the paper. This was the beginning of my mass media ride all the way to the front page of The Wall Street Journal."

"Thaddeus, did you have an agent?" "No and the book was self-published. That decision came about after realizing that no publisher would take a chance. My friend and mentor Khalil T. Adolemaiu-Bey, printing instructor at Carver Vocational High School, assisted and advised on getting this project camera ready. It wasn't easy; computers were few and far between then.

"Books were borrowed from the Enoch Pratt Free Library pertaining to self-publishing. My experiences as a professional salesman helped tremendously relative to making and introducing a product. Basically, my life savings were involved and my established goal was to recap my investment to its entirety. That was accomplished and more!

"Many bookstores in the City carried the book including Gordon's, B Dalton's and Greetings & Readings and was required reading at Community College of Baltimore and University of Baltimore. Personally, I was pleasantly shocked to observe when driving east on downtown's Baltimore Street and saw my books displayed throughout the showcase's entire front window of Gordon's Bookstore. Actually, I was flabbergasted! Even more so when the Schomburg Center for Research in Black Culture of the New York City Library requested copies for their permanent collection. That collection is the most prestigious in the country relative to America's Black Culture. Saying to myself, this is what it's all about. What an honor!

"The paperback versions sold in all of the City's 7/11 Stores. Baltimore City and Baltimore County Libraries purchased numerous copies of the publication. "*Hey Cabbie* was widely exposed to all segments of the mass media. Unfortunately, the social media was not available then. My goal was the global market. Primarily, cab patrons similarities are the same in most metropolitan cities worldwide!

"Advertising spaces were even purchased on the MTA Buses." "Really," she said. "There were many books sold personally, from sales pitches in the cab to book signing parties throughout the City. My downfall was burnout and being persuaded that *Hey Cabbie* was too local! But, my belief from dealing with human behaviors is that this could be any large metropolitan city in the world that deals with *the haves* and *the have nots*! But, I've really seen the world right here in Baltimore, you know!"

"That's enough about me and my book. What's your line of work or whatever?" "I've worked at the Social Security Administration over 30 years, downtown for the most part, got promoted recently to a higher supervisory position and was reassigned to Woodlawn. Also, I'm an avid reader, appreciate travel and adventure and have a daughter who's to marry soon." "That's wonderful."

"Hey, it's Friday evening." She was well coordinated and looked good. I've learned as a salesman to ask for the order. "What going on with you later?" "Nothing really." "Belvedere Square has an outdoor jazz concert. Would you be interested?" "Yes, that sounds good!" "How's 7:30PM? Cool, see you then. I'll pick up a good bottle of wine and bring my lawn chairs." She said, "Great, I'm looking forward to an enjoyable evening!"

Discussion Questions

1. What is your favorite story? Why?

2. What are the major themes/issues in the book? What examples does the author give to support them?

3. Can you point to specific stories that struck you personally as inspiring, illuminating, significant, amusing, disturbing, sad …?

4. How does the author feel about his job as a cab driver? What other roles/occupations/careers does he take on through his interactions with people and opinions about the City? What examples are there in the story to support your answers?

5. Were there situations and/or characters in the book that you can identify with, if so how?

6. Did you learn anything new reading this book? Did it broaden your perspective about an issue or situation? How has reading the book changed your opinion of persons or situations?

7. Who are the "haves" and the "have-nots"? How do they differ? How are they alike?

8. What is the current status of African American business, educational, recreational and/or cultural development in Baltimore?

9. How do the issues in the book affect your life? Directly, on a daily basis, in the future or more generally?

10. Does the author, or can you offer solutions to the problems or issues raised in the book? Who would implement those solutions? How probable is success?

ORDER INFORMATION

HEY CABBIE II

Price: $9.99
S & H: 3.00
Total: $12.99   Qty _____

HEY CABBIE

Price: $11.99
S & H: 3.00
Total: **$14.**99   Qty _____

SPECIAL: Buy both books for $25; get FREE shipping & handling.

Add 6% sales tax to your total order. Enclosed is my check or money order in the amount of $ _____ for _____ book(s).

Mail coupon with check or money order to:

Thaddeus Logan
PO Box 23465
Baltimore, MD 21203

www.HeyCabbie.net

Name: _____

Address: _____

City: _____

State/Zip Code: _____

Books make great gifts!
Allow 10-14 business days for delivery.

www.ingramcontent.com/pod-product-compliance
Lightning Source LLC
Chambersburg PA
CBHW051430280526
45785CB00003B/1238